"It's no surprise that Tony Rowe's book about a brilliant coaching career is so compelling. The book is an extension of the man himself - honest, warm, humorous and spiritually uplifting. Few high school running coaches in the United States have enjoyed as much success as Rowe, and it is fitting that such brilliance is so well-chronicled. "Trails, Trials and Triumphs" breasts the tape a clear-cut winner."

Jim Pickens
Sports Editor
Owensboro (Ky.) Messenger-Inquirer

D1607800

trails, **trials** *& triumphs*

— The Daviess County Running Tradition —

Tony **Rowe**

TATE PUBLISHING *& Enterprises*

TATE PUBLISHING
& Enterprises

For my wife, Pam;

our sons, Mark and Matt;

and

all of the young men who have competed

in a Daviess County jersey through the years.

— Acknowledgements —

To Obbie Todd for encouraging me to "just start writing" and all of your enthusiasm.

To Jenny Rightmyer, Debbie Sparks, Gail Kirkland, Sally James, Kim Menche, Karen Gaddis, Jim Pickens and Steve Rowe for your expert help and advice.

To all the parents, grandparents, and friends who have been so loyal to the Daviess County cross country program through the years.

To Jeff Arbogast for the kind words. I value your friendship.

To Art Harvey, Ken Willis, and the late Bob Puckett for instilling in me the love for the wonderful sport of cross country.

To my father and mother, Jim and Geneva Rowe for pouring your values into my life.

"To God be the glory!"

— Foreword —

If you have picked up a copy of Trails, Trials, and Triumphs, you are most likely one who feels just a bit different when the leaves start to fall and the air gets a cool crispness. You may still be double-knotting your spikes, or maybe that time has long since passed, but every year it inevitably hits you . . . it's racing season again! Some contextual clue in your life will give it away with rhythmic regularity. It's time for cross country!

Coach Tony Rowe's work that follows will touch each and every reader in some way. His overwhelming depth of experience is guaranteed to profoundly affect every athlete, coach, parent, and aficionado. As the Daviess County teams rise and fall and rise again, every one of us who values the lessons, camaraderie, and triumphs of this great sport will see within the pages of this book a representation of ourselves, albeit with different team colors and athlete names. You will exult with their triumphs and ache with their misfortunes, but within the teams that have passed under Coach Rowe, most importantly we see the athletes and people who mean the most to us in our own lives. Through the pages of this book pass the universal truths that govern excellence in all pure things, such as running three miles as fast as your will can power you.

The Daviess County teams are living out their dreams of determination under the tutelage of a man who has given his life to the development of young men of character. Humble, compassionate, and polite to a fault, Coach Rowe shows in a direct way how to mold youth to positive outcomes by detailing his learning experiences with meticulous precision. Yet after the 'art' of coaching is through, those looking for 'science' will find a treasure of information on the tactics that have made the Raging Red Line a fixture in the annals of prep cross country for decades. The 'art' is here, and the 'science' is here, but the reader of this book will gain the intangible . . . how to blend the two to create a cross country synergy that can jump-start your own team and resonate through your life.

Enjoy the heart and soul of this book, the unique inner workings of a season-to-season career masterpiece, but don't forget to transfer the lessons Coach Rowe has set on these pages to your own team, family, and life. Let his largest coaching experience be one of helping you to find a better way to coach, inspire, and mentor. From the first pages to the last, you will be captivated, just as this author has captivated the hearts of his team members, from first to last.

Jeff Arbogast

— Table of Contents —

I

— Introduction —

I consider myself the most blessed man in the world. The Lord has given me a wonderful wife, Pam, and two great sons, Mark and Matt. I wake up each day to a job that I greatly enjoy and one that helps shape young lives. Education is an incredible profession where the kids teach you as much as you do them. After school each day, I get to earn the title of "coach." I love it!

Running and racing is very basic, an almost natural instinct. As kids, we always wanted to see who was the fastest. For those of us who weren't quite as swift as our buddies, we began adding distance to the confrontations. I can remember leveling the playing field by issuing challenges of five and ten lappers around the house. I developed a passion for running the longer distances and finally got my first taste of cross country in 1968 as a high school freshman.

The sport has changed very little through the years. Sure, technology has made scoring and meet organization easier, and there are more and larger competitions. However, the simplicity and purity of cross country continues to amaze me. Train, go to the starting line, and get after it. Add up the total places of each team's top five runners and the low score wins. The challenge of the run itself is quite a test, but throw in the hills, the pace changes, the creek jumps, the competition . . . and the sport becomes extraordinary.

The aim of this manuscript is two-fold. First, I want to honor the young men who have given of themselves to the cross country program at Daviess County (Kentucky) High School through the years. Having kept extensive scrapbooks and summaries of each season, along with numerous e-mails, phone calls, and conversations, has given me the resources for mile splits, times, places, and recollections essential for accuracy.

My second goal is to share some simple training and motivational ideas that are components of our program. Some of those thoughts are sprinkled through the accounts of each season and many are in the special sections at the back of this book. Hopefully, coaches and runners can grab hold of a few principles that will broaden their knowledge and options for excelling over the hills and trails. Cross Country . . . lots of folks "just don't get it" until they get involved. It is then that the sport gets in your blood, and you begin to appreciate all that it has to offer.

II

— Early Tradition —

The Daviess County cross country roots can be traced back to 1965 when Paul Woodall coached the first Panther team. That very first year, Coach Woodall had a senior that loved to run and had an extraordinary work ethic to complement his talent. Allen Shouse lived out near Pleasant Ridge, more than ten miles from school. He would attend afternoon practice and then run home in time to do his evening chores on the family farm. At one point, he put in a 1,000 miles in just a few weeks. Talk about tough! The training paid off as Allen finished seventh in the Kentucky State Meet. After graduating, he served several years in the Air Force, continuing to train, and became a very elite distance runner. Allen represented the armed services in several international meets. The Air Force was prepared to release Allen from his base in Germany to return to the United States and train in preparation for the '72 Olympic Trials, when Allen felt the impression to go into the ministry. He weighed his priorities and decided he should devote himself to God's calling on his life.

Names like Billy Faith, Curtis Davidson, and Ken Draper headlined the cross country program in the years to follow, under the guidance of Coach Gary Imel. Then, in 1970, Chuck Gullo took the coaching position and was determined to turn the Daviess County program into one of the state's elite. It didn't take long. In the '71 state meet, about ten yards from the finish line, Tom Edwards of Greensburg looked over his right shoulder, sensing someone was catching him. Curtis Hopewell sprinted past him on the left, becoming Daviess County's first individual state champion. It was a big day for the red and white as Virgil Davidson came home third, Ardell Hanley fourth, Ron Berry fifth, and Norman

DeCaussin 35th, resulting in Daviess County's first team state championship. In '72 the Panthers defended that title, placing Davidson second, Roger Holeman eighth and freshman Billy Moorman ninth. Moorman's outstanding career saw him have an astounding four top ten finishes at state, culminated by a brilliant romp in '75 when he became the second individual state champion for the Panthers.

III

— Taking the Reins–The Late 70's —

In mid August of 1977, I was lying in a hospital bed recovering from surgery, when the phone rang. My mom was on the other end of the line and said that the Daviess County school system had called, wanting me to come in for an interview. Coach Chuck Gullo had taken a job at Fort Thomas Highlands in Northern Kentucky, leaving the boys cross country/track and field job open at Daviess County High School. I had already signed to begin my first teaching/coaching position with some fine folks in Bourbon County, near Lexington. However, the opportunity to coach in my hometown, even if it were at the rival school from which I graduated and against whom I competed, seemed to be too good to pass up. The next morning, a Friday, I was released from the hospital. That afternoon, after going through a rigorous three hour interview process, I was told that the job was mine if I wanted it, but I would have to work out the situation with Bourbon County. Apprehensively, I called their superintendent and he very graciously freed me from my contract. The following Monday I began working with the Daviess County boys cross country team. The program I inherited already had a legacy of success. Realizing I had some big shoes to fill, my goal was to continue the tradition of excellence that Paul Woodall, Gary Imel and Chuck Gullo before me had initiated.

Coaching Philosophy

Every coach needs solid, specific goals that steer the direction of his or her program. When I was in high school, I came across a very simple, yet profound quote. It stated, "A man becomes a champion by working harder than the other fellow!" I wrote it down in my scrapbook of meet clippings, and those words have been a part of who I am ever since. I was blessed to see work ethic exemplified in my father, who was one of the hardest workers I have ever seen, as well as my mother. The two coaches whom I spent most of my competition days under were Bob Puckett at Owensboro High School and Art Harvey at Eastern Kentucky University. Boy, did they put us through some workouts! These two men reinforced what my parents taught me and impacted my life so powerfully during those special years. I did not win many races individually, but I certainly learned profound lessons about the importance of team and the value of effort.

The second part of my coaching philosophy is this: God has given everyone talents. It is our responsibility to develop those gifts He has placed within us and honor Him by the way we practice, compete, act, react, win, and lose. I tell my runners that God has given them the talent to run . . . what a privilege! There are kids in our school in wheelchairs that would give nearly anything to be able to even get up and take a single step. Giving our best is the very least we should do!

"For in Him we live, and move, and have our being . . ." Acts 17:28

— 1977 —

As we met at Hillcrest Golf Course for practice on August 17, 1977, I thought it appropriate to begin with a little meeting to introduce myself and get to know the boys. After a few words, McKay Mattingly, who would become my first state champion, said, "Coach, you might want to move over on this side so John can see you." I found out that John Dickinson, who apparently was distracted and looking in another direction, was deaf. Chuck Gullo had not warned me about this. John, however, read lips very well and communication was not much of a problem. The other guys picked on John during the season but John brought much of it on himself. However, for the most part we all got along very well.

When I Knew

Our first invitational of my rookie coaching season was one that I will never forget. The meet went well, with McKay Mattingly finishing first and Scott Eckstein fourth and the team placing very high overall. However, it was moments earlier, during the girls' race while my guys were warming up, that I was overwhelmed with emotion. Our girls' team, coached by Willie Pagan, was sprinting toward the finish chute when my eyes literally filled with tears. Somehow, the setting, seeing their effort, and the passion that I have for the sport all hit me at once. It was a special moment, as if God was confirming in my very spirit that this was what I was intended to do. I felt very, very blessed to have been placed in this position. I have embraced that passion day after day and year after year ever since, for this . . . the very purest of all sports.

Leader of the Pack

Early in the season, we were in Northern Kentucky for the Covington Catholic Invitational. After checking into the hotel on Friday evening, we went to Camp Marydale to run over the course. John Dickinson liked to act as a tour guide for the team at the sites where he had previously run. As usual, he bolted out in front, muttering something about knowing the way. One of the guys said, "Let's hide," and I played along. John finally looked back and saw that his team was nowhere to be found. After several seconds of pleading with them, the guys emerged from their hiding places. It didn't break John's desire to be team guide, but he was careful to keep an eye on his teammates after that.

Cross-Town Rivals

I suppose it was natural for Owensboro to be our main rival during my first year of coaching. Owensboro had won five state championships in the late 60's and early 70's. I ran on three of those teams. It was Daviess County that broke a string of four straight class AA state championships for Owensboro in '71 and followed that with another championship in '72, before Owensboro reclaimed the title in '73. It was a great era for cross country in our town. I was accused of still having a bit of red and black blood when I took the Daviess County position, but I can tell you that it only took me about one day of being with my team to commit 100% loyalty to the program.

It seemed like Owensboro showed up everywhere we went that year. We ran them, heads up, in thirteen different meets. We had defeated

Owensboro eight times and they had beaten us in three meetings as we headed into the Western Kentucky Regional (state meet qualifier). We had an advantage over them in meets with large numbers because our top two runners were finishing so high. Owensboro's strength was a tight pack. We worked through the week of the region. I sent a somewhat tired team to the starting line and paid the price! Although Mattingly and Eckstein finished first and third that day, Owensboro got the best of us, winning 35 to 43. Call it a rookie mistake! I knew we would have to be much more rested for state a week later.

State Meet '77

The first state meet I coached was held in a large field across from Commonwealth (football) Stadium at the University of Kentucky, in Lexington. The butterflies in my stomach were not much different than when I was a competitor in '69, '70, and '71. Those suckers get bigger and bigger in the hype leading up to the start of the race. By the time you are standing on the line, it feels like your stomach is turning flips. Learning how to handle that part of the event is extremely important, and experience really does make a difference. A runner's psyche can easily be blown with all the pre-race hoopla. That is an important reason why we try to get our guys to focus on the team rather than themselves. Once the starter's gun is fired the jitters go away. It's such a relief to finally get on with that for which you have trained. Physical control is often easier to harness than emotional control.

What to wear . . . what to wear?

I suppose if you have never been to a cross country meet, deciding the appropriate attire can be confusing. About one month after I began my coaching career, I met Pam Henderson at Maceo Elementary School, where I was teaching. Pam's mom was the secretary there, and Pam would come out and eat lunch with her from time to time. Our first date, of sorts, was at a cross country meet. The day I met Pam, I invited her to come out and watch a meet we were hosting that very afternoon. Pam and Mrs. Henderson soon became cross country fans and saw many of our meets in the fall of '77. I was excited that the two of them, along with Pam's aunt, Jessie, were making the three hour drive from Owensboro to see the state meet. This would be Jessie's rookie meet as a spectator, and she was in for a real cross country education. Between trying to trudge through the mud in her fancy pant suit and high heels and seeing guys slip, slide, fall, vomit and all the other normal happenings that go on in our sport, Jessie just wasn't real impressed. She went away muttering something about it being "cruel and disgusting." Jessie has since become a loyal cross country supporter, but no longer wears high heels to meets!

Our team wore the appropriate attire, but we were a bit rag-tag. When I took on the program earlier that fall, I didn't inherit much in the way of sweat suits or a budget. As a matter of fact, we would have been hard to identify as a team during the warm-up. One of our guys had light blue sweats, another orange; still another was in red and dark blue, while the other four wore an assortment of red and white, which are actually our school colors. Fortunately, I was able to scrape together enough identical jerseys and shorts for us to be legal during the competition.

The race itself in those days was two miles. Kentucky did not lengthen the distance for boys to 5,000 meters (3.1 miles) until 1978. In a two mile race late in the season, when competitors are sharp, there just was not much room for mistakes. It really did favor runners with good strength and speed. Junior McKay Mattingly had those tools. I sent him to the starting line along with seniors Joel Ray and Sam Wilson, juniors Scott Eckstein, George Weatherholt, and John Dickinson, sophomore Mike Rhodes, and freshman Brian Autry. With Mattlingly (2nd) and Eckstein (7th) leading the way, we came home with a solid third place effort . . . two spots ahead of Owensboro.

Silence Is Golden

The 1977 season was followed by a challenging winter. We do not receive an extreme amount of snow in Western Kentucky and we don't handle the white stuff very well. A half inch of the frosty precipitation can actually close schools around these parts. When several snowfalls and an extended spell of very cold weather graced our landscape in the winter of 1977–78, activity really slowed down. Still, I spent quite a bit of time heading up Highway 60 toward Lindy Lane as my relationship with Pam Henderson became more and more serious. Pam was outgoing, intelligent, fun to be around and beautiful. I felt very comfortable with Pam. When we were not together, I found myself constantly daydreaming about her. In late winter, being a victim to Cupid's most potent arrow, I visited a local jeweler and prepared to pop the question.

On a frigid Thursday evening, with the ring tucked safely into the glove compartment of my '69 Chevy, I picked up Pam and we headed toward the nearby community of Thruston. The solitude of Yellow Creek Park, laced in a fresh layer of snow, would be a beautiful and romantic site to ask Pam to share the rest of our lives together.

About a quarter of a mile down the road into the park, I decided that although the engagement idea was a winner, the park idea might put a frozen damper on the evening. I slowed to a stop, put the ole' Chevy in reverse, and proceeded to get hopelessly stuck in the snow. After several minutes of spinning tires but going nowhere, Pam and I trudged away from the stranded vehicle to the nearby home of Ted and Eva Peercy, an older couple who were members of the church I had attended most of my life.

Ted answered my knock on the door and I stammered and stuttered through what sounded like a contrived tale of why we were stuck in the park on a night such as this. I'm not sure the Peercy's believed the engagement story. Still, Ted was kind enough to get his tractor and chain and take me back to the park to retrieve my car.

Back at the Peercy's I picked up Pam, who had kept Eva company for quite some time, and we headed back to her parent's home. There, in the driveway, I pulled out the package and Pam made my evening perfect by agreeing to become my wife.

We went inside and I chose just the right moment (the three minutes between *Three's Company* and another sitcom) to present my best "may I have your daughter's hand in marriage" spiel to Pam's parents. It went something like this.

"There's something that I'd like to–uh–ask you all. You know that Pam and I–uh–we love each other and–uh–we want to spend the rest of our–uh–lives together and well–uh–I'd like to–uh–have your permission to marry . . . Pam." How eloquent!

Pam's father said nothing.

Her mom responded, "You can marry her on one condition."

"Uh—what's that?" I asked.

"You have to bring her back home every Sunday afternoon for dinner." Understand here that Bettie Henderson is one of the world's best cooks and I'm always up for a good meal.

"I can do that!"

Pam's father said nothing.

After an awkward moment of wondering, I looked at Mrs. Henderson and inquired, "Is this alright with him too?" nodding toward Bobby Henderson.

"If it wasn't he would tell you," she replied.

Pam's father said nothing . . . but after a few seconds he took off his glasses and wiped a tear away. It may have been a tear of regret, but I took it as a "yes."

On June 24th of 1978, in front of "God and these witnesses" (which included several of my runners), Pam wore her beautiful wedding gown as she walked down the aisle of Maceo Baptist Church. When the moment of truth arrived the Reverend Randy Jones asked, "Who gives this woman to be married to this man?" Bobby Henderson broke the silence with a reassuring "her mother and I" . . . and I became the happiest man in the world.

— 1978 —

Water Anyone?

The Covington Catholic Invitational seemed to bring out the best . . . or worst . . . in John Dickinson. We had finished our Friday evening jog over the Covington course, and I had called for the team to meet in one of our hotel rooms. I walked in and sat down in a chair. Most of the team was already in the room, and we were having some casual conversation when there was a knock at the door. One of the guys opened the door to find a security officer and two young ladies all dolled up. One of the girls, however, had wet spots on her clothes, and her hair was pretty much drenched. The officer asked, "Who is in charge of this group?" The boys said nothing but several of them pointed at me. You can imagine what scenarios were going through my mind. About that time, McKay Mattingly, who had been showering and did not know we had company, walked out of the bathroom wearing only a towel (thank goodness he had that much on!). The wet girl was madder than a hornet and threatening all kinds of things with phrases that were interspersed with words like "arrest" and "jail." I was clueless as to what had happened but assumed that our three fine visitors must have thought some of our guys were the culprits.

As it turned out, they were right. Unknown to me, the guys had been having a little water tossing game. John Dickinson was the main victim. A couple of teammates called and had John sent to one of the other rooms. When he knocked on the door, they opened it and threw a cup of water on him. The little game began to escalate, and finally John decided he would have the last laugh. He filled up the trash can in his room with water and waited. When he sensed one of the guys was outside his door, John threw it open, slung the water, and quickly slammed the door shut. Our rooms were on the second floor with outside entrances. The water missed its intended victim and went over the balcony. These two unsuspecting girls, ready for a big night out, were walking into the motel lounge below and . . . now you can make the connection! After several moments of her ranting and raving and my apologizing, the young lady began to calm down, and we offered her the only thing that could make a difference at the time . . . a hairdryer!

Raging Red Line

The guys decided we needed a nickname . . . a team handle, if you will. Someone suggested "The Long Red Line" after reading about Elmhurst York, Illinois', "Long Green Line." Too much similarity! "The Raging Red" had a unique ring to it, and finally the guys amended the suggestion to "Raging Red Line." The team adopted the phrase and had shirts printed up to that effect. Little did they realize that nearly thirty years later, Daviess County teams would still refer to themselves by that nickname.

A Missed Opportunity

The development of Mike Rhodes through his sophomore year and the following summer was very encouraging. By the time the '78 season began, it looked as if our top three of seniors McKay Mattingly and Scott Eckstein, along with Rhodes, would give us a very potent punch up front. Brian Autry, a gutsy and feisty little sophomore, would be a solid fourth man. Seniors Dickinson, Mike Linville, and George Weatherholt gave us the depth to make a run for the state title.

As the season unwound, Mattingly and Eckstein began reaping the benefits of the 70 and 80 mile weeks they logged during much of the summer, with McKay winning race after race and Scott nipping at his heels. Great runners set the bar high and inspire their teammates, who become much better themselves. Such was the case with our team. By October, Mike Rhodes had blossomed into a legitimate front runner himself and actually tied McKay and Scott in the Big Eight Conference meet, all three running 16:12 (5,000 meters). A few days later, in the Lexington Catholic Invitational on the State Meet course, McKay, Mike, and Scott ran 15:16, 15:53, and 15:54, respectively. Suddenly, we had three guys with aspirations of finishing in the top five at state. Brian Autry's running had also been greatly impacted by his swift training partners. By mid-season there was not another team in Kentucky whose #4 man could handle Brian.

We did suffer a slight setback in late September when Weatherholt was diagnosed with a stress fracture in his foot and missed several weeks of solid training. However, Dickinson or Linville usually closed our scoring in quick order, and the team was on a late season roll until another incident struck a blow two weeks before the regional. Autry, solid on the course but unpredictable off of it, got involved in a scuffle at school and wound up with a cracked kneecap. He would spend the remainder of the fall with his leg in a cast. Still, we dethroned Owensboro as regional champs with Weatherholt proving to be the comeback kid, finishing as our #4 man. Our top five ran 1, 2, 3, 9, 10 (25 points), and we were very confident one week later as we headed for the Kentucky Horse Park, a new state meet site near Lexington.

The state course was basically two and a half large loops around a horse steeplechase area. The layout had no major hills but rolled enough to consistently challenge the runners. Trying to master a new course and the competition, however, were not the only challenges. The runners were already acclimatized to the cooler late fall temperatures. State meet day '78 dawned much warmer than normal, and by race time it was quickly heading toward 80 degrees. Sometimes confidence needs to be tempered with a little wisdom; this was one of those times. Backing off the early pace a bit would've been the smartest plan.

Mattingly and Eckstein merely did what they had done all season . . . race at the front. Rhodes, with newfound confidence over the last half of the season, matched them stride for stride. As the race progressed, our top three guys were running perhaps their best collective effort of the season, and our #4-#7 runners were well packed somewhere around 45th to 50th place. Autry, who I felt would have had a good shot at the top 30, was anxiously watching from the sidelines, giving his cast a good workout. At the 4,000 meter mark there was a lead pack of five runners, three of whom wore Daviess County red.

Being a NASCAR fan, I know that a hot rod needs to keep all of its tires on to win a race, and two of ours were about to go flat. The heat and hot pace caught up to both Eckstein and Rhodes about the same time, and the last kilometer was some kind of struggle for them. Most runners have been in that nightmare zone where the mindset goes from pure excitement to trying to survive. Scott Eckstein and Mike Rhodes began to fade. Both developed heat problems with Eckstein collapsing as he crossed the finish line, just ahead of his teammate. To their credit, each still had decent finishes of 11th and 12th. As for McKay Mattingly, he culminated a dominant season with an impressive state meet win.

We knew the team chase was close as Erlanger Lloyd had moved up well late in the race. I was anxious to congratulate McKay, and it took a while to track him down in the crowd and excitement surrounding the finish area. When I finally found him, McKay looked at me and said, "Sorry." Apparently, he already knew what I was to find out officially just moments later. Lloyd had run the race of their season, taking advantage of our mistakes, and beat us 93–97. Four points isn't much in a cross country race, but it was the difference on this day in the gold and silver trophies. Looking back on McKay's reaction, I realized just how much the team meant to him. I am certain he would have traded that individual title for a team championship without blinking an eye. That's the kind of attitude you want on your team.

The Kinney/Footlocker Cross Country Championships was not initiated until two years later, in 1980. However, I believe with all my heart that McKay would have become a national qualifier in that program. He had the unique blend of talent, strength, smooth speed, work ethic, and competitiveness that separates great runners from the good ones, and those qualities served him well. McKay put together a string of twelve straight wins during his outstanding senior year.

Scott Eckstein (603), McKay Mattingly (602), and Mike Rhodes (604) in the lead pack at the 1978 state meet.

— 1979 —

Coming so close to winning state in '78 whetted our team appetite for a big-time win. Losing five of our top seven to graduation, however, painted a very clear picture that could be titled, *Rebuilding Year.* Senior Mike Rhodes looked to be one of the state's best, and a healthy Brian Autry was a good sign. After those two we would have to depend on youth and inexperience for the desired team success.

We battled in-town rival Apollo for local supremacy all season long. We couldn't get away from them, so there was never a break from tough competition. The frequent challenges had their rewards. As the fall progressed, both teams seemed destined for good finishes on the state level. We could beat Apollo up front, but they had a super pack and at times put seven men in front of our fifth. Indeed, in early October at the Lincoln Trail Invitational, Craig Hopkins' team beat us by eight points, our first loss to Apollo in several years. We bounced back with an eight point win over them in the Big Eight Conference meet, the last regular season race, setting up a showdown for the regional a week later.

If coaching were simply developing workouts, taping ankles, planning race strategies, driving buses, purchasing equipment, sending in entry forms, hosting meets, preparing meet itineraries, writing out meet summaries, grooming your home course, dealing with public relations . . . we would have it made. But no, it's not that simple! We also have to be a surrogate parent, psychologist, and disciplinarian. How could you predict that your number four runner, who literally dove across the finish line at conference trying to pick up a place, would decide to skip practice on the day before the regional championship? Had he not run at conference, we would have come away with a five point loss, rather than an eight point win. Even though it was championship season, I had to hold the young man out. I wasn't looking forward to battling Apollo shorthanded, but coaches should never seek wins by sacrificing principles.

Beat 'em to the Water Fountain

We were to host the regional at Hillcrest Golf Course, just down the road from our school. The layout basically rimmed the perimeter of the property two times. I decided that we needed to be very aggressive and put the pressure on Apollo to try and catch us. The two mile mark was right in front of a water fountain on the second loop, near the back side of the course. Our goal became to run like it was a two mile race, beating them to the water fountain and toughing out the last mile. The guys stepped it up and executed the plan perfectly. The quick pace seemed to catch everybody else by surprise and they never caught up. Mike Rhodes (1st), junior Brian Autry (3rd), and sophomore Jerry Weihe (4th) supplied our punch up front. Freshman Jimmy Evans came through with a huge race, infiltrating the Apollo pack and finishing 13th in a fine time of 17:32. With senior Tim Frost, better known for his pole vaulting exploits, finishing 17th, our 38 points translated into a 13 point victory. Adversity brought out the best in our guys.

State Meet '79

State meet was a learning experience for me. When the season began, I did not expect that we would be in contention for the championship. Yet, ten weeks later no team was absolutely dominant, and our chances of a high finish looked good. I continued to work our team hard through the middle of the week preceding State, and we felt ready for the challenge on the steeplechase loops of the Horse Park. Ironically, the meet would come down to Chuck Gullo's Fort Thomas Highlands squad and us. Chuck, of course, had been my predecessor at Daviess County and now was taking dead aim at a state title at his second school.

Mike Rhodes paced the Panthers with a nice fifth place effort, followed by Weihe (22nd), Autry (29th), junior Gregg Smith (35th), and Evans (73rd), but it seemed that we ran very sluggishly. Gullo's team low scored us 99–124. For the second straight year Daviess County earned the team runner-up trophy, which, at the beginning of the season, we might have been thrilled with. As I reflected on the meet and the workouts leading up to the race, I realized that our guys competed tired. In a championship environment, every ache, pain, and tense muscle is amplified in the mind of teen-age athletes. Just like in '78, we let a championship slip away, and I had to take the blame for this one. A significant lesson was reinforced that day about the value of sending your horses to the gate with fresh legs. Coaching is a continuous learning experience and often agonizing process, but what a profession it is!

IV

— Adding to Tradition–The 80's —

— 1980 —

Boxing

Pam and I had been married for just over two years when summer training began in '80. We lived in the Maceo area, a farming community in the far eastern part of the county, as did several young men on our squad. They would ride home from the high school with me after practice, and we soon found a form of cross-training to pass the time while waiting for parents to pick them up.

I happened to have a pair of boxing gloves. The rules were simple. Put one glove on and the bare hand behind your back, and have some testosterone-driven fun. The sparring escalated when someone came up with a second pair of gloves, and it wasn't long until guys that lived nowhere near Maceo were showing up.

It seemed that every one of them felt that their rite of passage into manhood was to take on the coach (yours truly) in this fine art of pugilism. Senior Keith Creager, a strapping 6'1" lad, made a special trip out to join the festivities one day and, of course, wanted to see what I was made of. After a light exchange of warm-up punches, I made the mistake of spreading my hands and exposing my face. Keith absolutely drilled me with a right cross. You've heard of seeing stars. I am here to tell you that there were dozens of little swirlies, a display fit for the Fourth of July, right in front of my eyes. When I was cognizant enough to understand words again, my exuberant opponent said, "Me and my dad box all the time down in our basement, but he won't let me hit him in the face!" The kid could have given Sugar Ray Leonard a run for his money.

I finally had to put a stop to the brawling because guys were coming to practice with extra aches and pains, and it was interfering with their workouts. At least, that's the excuse I used . . . truth is, I was getting tired of being whipped on all the time.

Defections

We were really looking forward to another exciting cross country season, but some major defections left us very young and inexperienced. Jerry Weihe moved to Louisville. Gregg Smith was still recovering from a compound fracture of his lower leg from a pole vaulting accident during track season. A very promising sophomore decided to forego cross country to concentrate on basketball. Three others had a parting of the ways with us for different reasons. These young men would possibly have been our top six, and all were capable of very good state meet finishes. I was fairly distraught but the season had to continue. Guys who should have been gaining experience in junior varsity races were thrust into varsity roles. Junior Jeff O'Bryan and sophomore Dennis Brown headed to the point of our pack, but midway through the season we took another hit when Dennis had a freak accident at home, severely spraining an ankle. His conditioning would never completely catch up. We certainly took our fair share of lickings during a very trying campaign, but had a fun and hard-working group of young men whose efforts began to pay off by late season.

The best performance of the '80 team came in the regional meet, where the top two teams would advance to state. One week prior, in the six team conference meet, Owensboro, running without their number two man, beat us by 28 points and quickly improving Owensboro Catholic bested us by 20 points. As a matter of fact, every team in the regional meet had beaten us at least once during the season. The very young team we sent to the starting line included senior Keith Creager, juniors O'Bryan and Brad Jagoe, as well as a still gimpy Dennis Brown and fellow sophomores Kevin Marsch, Darren Christian and Richard Bowen. As expected, Owensboro won the regional crown with 53 points, edging Catholic by two. Our 64 points, without Brown in the scoring mix, earned the third spot. Our truly tested guys fell only 10 points shy of earning a state berth and a mere 12 points away from being outright regional champions. To this day, I still look back at this group and smile, believing this to be one of the better efforts given through all my years of coaching. Even though we did not qualify for state, all the adversity that the '80 team endured developed a toughness that served as a great foundation for what would be our first team state championship two years later. The extra year of varsity experience for some of our younger guys truly turned into a blessing.

— 1981 —

Every cross country campaign is special. We have goals, opportunities, and we have seniors for whom there will not be a next year, as far as high school running is concerned. While we try to maximize the performances and results of every season, some turn into transitional years. In '81 we were a year away from having the front runners necessary to make a serious charge at a state title, yet we were able to put together some good races at opportune times and whip some of the top dogs around.

A great boost to our team strength was the addition of junior Scott Katchuk, who moved to Daviess County from upstate New York. Scott was a fairly high-spirited young man with decent speed and strength. The very amiable crew at hand readily accepted Scott; his greatest adjustments were trying to decipher our Kentucky accents and getting through the steamy summer of training.

We eased into the season with a couple of dual meets before tackling the Jasper, Indiana Invitational where Bloomington (Indiana) South, clearly the best team we faced in '81, put on a clinic. The Jasper course had a painfully steep and long hill that caused many unprepared runners to commit the "w" word . . . walk! It may have been the toughest hill I've seen on a cross country course and our guys nicknamed it "atomic hill."

Nonetheless, we seemed well prepared for our first significant in-state invitational at Shelby County a week later. We came back with an encouraging seven point win over Louisville Trinity and a 19 point margin over tough local rival Owensboro. We rode that wave right into a good spanking by the same two teams and several others at the Covington Catholic Invitational. That's the way the season seemed to go, good one meet and somewhat marginal the next. Still, I was encouraged by the development of our team. We were gaining some quality depth and our junior varsity was in the midst of an exceptional year.

The late season was certainly not sensational, but we were able to finish as regional runners-up to a very strong Owensboro squad. A new classification system placed us in the same division with all of the largest schools in Kentucky, and we finished sixth in the Class AAA State Meet.

Champion Louisville Trinity and runner-up Owensboro were teams we had certainly mixed it up well with at times during the season. Scott Katchuk continued his tendency of competing well in the big meets, finishing 21st. Dennis Brown was next in for the Panthers, in 49th, followed by fellow juniors Darren Christian (60th) and Richard Bowen (63rd). Promising freshman Dean Roberts (67th) closed out our scoring with Dane Allen and Kevin Marsch also gaining state meet experience. With all seven coming back and several young bucks ready to challenge them for position, the groundwork had been laid for exciting days ahead.

— 1982 —

After having some decent success during my first four seasons, we entered the '82 campaign with high expectations. From the first day of practice, the maturity and talent of our senior-dominated squad gave indications of a special season ahead. Scott Katchuk was significantly stronger than the previous year, but Dennis Brown was now setting the pace in most of our workouts. Dennis was a laid-back country boy who had transformed into a very reliable leader and a competitor that belied his calm personality. Another surprise came in the form of David Douglas, who had played football the previous three years and specialized as a half-miler each spring. His easy adjustment to the rigors of the hills and trails indicated David would make an immediate impact for us. By the time our first meet rolled around, we were ready to go out and take no prisoners.

(1. to r.) Kevin Clark, Darren Christian, and David Douglas were part of the strong Daviess County attack in 1982.

Getting Priorities Straight

There's certainly nothing wrong with winning as long as it is done the right way, but it is very easy to get so wrapped up in it that priorities get out of whack. I must admit that mine were probably headed that way.

After winning several early-season meets, we were handed a setback at the New Albany (Indiana) Invitational, on a beautiful Friday evening. We were very lethargic, placing third, and I was plain 'ole aggravated. I left there anxious to put the team back on the starting line for the next race. We would not have to wait long because I had scheduled us to compete in the Antioch Invitational the very next day.

We hopped on the bus and began the three hour ride down I-65 to Nashville. By the time we got there and ate at Pizza Hut, it was well after one o'clock in the morning. I was anxious to see how the guys would respond to the late night trip and doubling up with back to back meets. They didn't let me down! There were thirty-one full teams that showed up at Percy Warner Park that Saturday morning, and our guys ran a very spirited race with seniors Dennis Brown (2nd-15:44) and Scott Katchuk (3rd-15:53) leading the way. Our next three guys came across the line in the 15th, 20th, and 26th positions, and our low score of 61 points (after taking non-scoring individuals out) won the meet. I learned a lot about our team that day, but I learned even more from Bobby Parsley.

Before the meet, people were talking about Bobby and what a talented runner he was. I made it a point to observe him throughout the morning. Bobby's shirt immediately drew my attention. It had the scripture from Isaiah 40:31 screened on the back that says, "But they that wait upon the Lord shall renew their strength; they shall mount up with wings as eagles; they shall run, and not be weary; and they shall walk, and not faint." As a Christian, I was intrigued by this. The young man must have intentionally had the shirt printed up because this was before most Christian bookstores offered those type shirts.

As runners were herded to their starting boxes, Bobby took his position somewhere near one of the far ends of the starting line. Bobby was from Unicoi County High School over in East Tennessee; they did not even have enough runners to field a scoring team. Almost as soon as the starter's pistol sounded, Bobby bolted to the lead and smoothly sailed through the three miles in 15:39, winning handily. After all the dust settled, I made it a point to find Bobby and talk with him. I will never forget the special spirit he had and how he humbly and genuinely credited God for his talent and success.

Driving the bus home, I began to re-evaluate my own priorities. A few years after that, we began to wear scriptures on the back of our team warm-up shirts, and the practice spread to other teams in our area. We have often been asked by different people at the various meets we compete in how we are able to get by with Bible quotes on our shirts since we are a public school. I suppose the answer is that no one has ever told us we could not, and honoring the one who gives us every good and perfect gift we have is the right thing to do. I just wish Bobby Parsley could know the far-reaching effects that his simple desire to glorify God has had. Winning is much more than crossing the finish line first!

Our First State Championship—The Eyes Have It!

Sometimes, you just know! We went into the state meet of '82 as the prohibitive favorite. We had not been beaten by another Kentucky team all season and rolled through the Regional one point shy of perfection, going 1–2–3–4–6 for 16 points. That kind of success can breed two qualities . . . confidence and cockiness. I always want my teams to be very confident, knowing they have prepared well and ready to carry out a smart race plan. It's basically a matter of 16 or 17 minutes of doing what you've done all season, but a bit better. Bringing the kids up to that certain mindset without teetering over the edge is the key. We've all seen overconfidence become a liability resulting in a flat, disappointing performance. I was anxious to see what the pre-race team huddle might reveal. Looking at each runner, I saw the same thing: determination. The guys had a job to do and their eyes showed they were ready to embrace the task. In that huddle, under a very overcast sky, I knew we were moments away from capturing our first state championship of my coaching era.

By 1200 meters we were well packed and solidly winning the race. As the guys passed me, I told them (actually screamed at them) to hold their place and we would win the meet. They did! Senior Scott Katchuk, who really came on late in the season, led us across the line with a fourth place finish. David Douglas (14th), Dennis Brown (17th), Richard Bowen (26th), and Dean Roberts (27th) finished up our scoring with Darren Christian (37th) and Kevin Clark (40th) close behind. I was too excited to pay much attention to the steady rain that began to fall. I'll never forget running toward the finish area after our last guy crossed the line. Each step was something between a run, a hop and about a ten foot high jump off the ground. At least, that's what it felt like. There's nothing like the feeling of knowing that the team has won the state championship!

On a very personal note, Pam was five months pregnant with our first son, Mark. I don't know that the excitement of the season had anything to do with it, but Mark sure was anxious to join the fun. He was born just a few weeks later, three months ahead of schedule, weighing in at a whopping two pounds. After spending the first eighty or so days of his life in a neo-natal center, Mark finally got to come home with us. Not surprisingly, he developed a great passion for running from a very early age.

Scott Katchuk (1. front) and Dennis Brown ponder their 1982 state meet race. Jimmy Evans, Dean Roberts and Steve Payne are in the background.

The 1982 team hoists their state championship trophy.

— 1983 —

Inexperience!?

I have always felt that when guys have been in our program a couple of years and it is their time to step up to varsity, they suddenly become much better runners. Maybe it's just maturity or the expectations to carry on tradition, or perhaps it's the confidence gained from earning a top seven spot. In truth, I am sure there are many factors, but it is neat to observe.

Losing five of the men that ran at state in '82, only Dean Roberts and Kevin Clark returned. Our junior varsity of the past couple of years, however, had been very impressive. I figured we would lose a few early season tussles and improve over the course of the season, but the guys sprang out of the gate with a surprising intensity. At the Antioch Invitational in Nashville on September 17th, the best team in Tennessee, Oak Ridge, and the defending state champions from Georgia, Walton, slipped by us. Those were the only two teams that got our measure through the first seven meets.

We were a junior-dominated squad, and our leaders on the course were Dean Roberts and Bill Dechman, both very bright young men, but with very different personalities. Dean was introspective and quiet. Bill was very outgoing and always ready for conversation, trivial or otherwise. Bill was one of those easily excited guys, and he always had a newfound motivational quote to share.

Our young men were not sensational, but were certainly a tough-minded unit that thrived on toil and perspiration. Deon Baize epitomized that mindset. He had certainly endured more adversity than your normal high school senior. Deon did not live with his family, but resided in a local motel with a 25 year old guardian that attended his church. Each day seemed to bring a new test, but Deon never saw himself as a victim. His attitude was that of finding a way to "get it done." Deon told me early in the season, "I'm not a runner; I'm a worker!"

Deon wasn't the only worker. Kevin Clark, Steve Payne, Kenny Linville, guys that had been in the program a while, reflected the same virtue. A valuable addition came in the form of Tom Dycus, who had moved in over the summer from Southern Indiana. His positive, gregarious nature was a great asset, and Tom seemed so appreciative to be a part of us. He had been somewhat under-trained, but after a good chunk of "feet hitting the pavement," the runner inside him began to emerge.

The second half of the season began with three tough invitationals. We finished second in the Lincoln Trail meet to Floyd Central, probably the best team in Southern Indiana. Next was a tough competition at the Horse Park, where we trailed St. Xavier, Oak Ridge, and Lincoln (Ohio) to the finish line. Bill Dechman came up with his finest performance of the year after reading a story about engineers studying bumblebees. Apparently, there is no physiological reason why bumblebees should be able to fly, yet they defy logic. Bill, the ever excitable one, decided that he too would take wing, running a 16:40 personal best and finishing fifth out of 252 competitors. If only he could've bottled that psyche and taken a drink before every race! A week later came the five hour trek to compete in the Oak Ridge Invitational. The East Tennessee mountains are a beautiful setting for a cross country race. We edged the defending Tennessee state champs, Christian Brothers, but Oak Ridge, Knoxville Farragut and a gradual mile long climb that graced the course, sent us back to Western Kentucky in third place.

We were in need of some confidence building performances in the next three meets, prepping for state. The guys took advantage of the first opportunity by running a very aggressive last two miles and triumphed in the thirty-nine team Pulaski County Invitational. We lost some potency, however, when Deon Baize, who developed a real consistency and had run as high as third man on the team, couldn't overcome a nagging injury that would sideline him for the remainder of the season. A few days later Roberts, Dechman, and Clark led us to a conference title on a rain-soaked turf at Yellow Creek Park. Surprising Madisonville, on the strength of a one-two punch of Fred Rorer and Austin Dean, ran a stout second. With the meet slated to be contested on their home course, the Maroons had ideas about dethroning us as regional champions a week later.

No Need to Panic

Madisonville coach Cindy Fitch had the regional layout well-groomed and sprinkled with colorful balloons and streamers, a real fall festival type atmosphere. Once the race began, however, their guys were anything but hospitable. A couple of hundred yards off the starting line, the course suddenly tapered, becoming a very narrow trail for the better part of the first mile. The home team took advantage of knowing how to run their course, getting out very aggressively. By the time we were able to find room to pass people, the Maroons had a considerable gap over our seven. The pressure was on and I began to get in panic mode. In other words, I was running from point to point and squawking like a madman! We were not able to penetrate their group until early in the third mile. Even paced running is actually the most efficient use of energy, but it takes young athletes with a bundle of confidence to buy into that type of race. In reality, getting slowed down the first mile probably acted in our favor. Madisonville's dynamic duo of Rorer and Dean repeated their conference performance in the first two spots. However, Dean Roberts, Bill Dechman, and Kevin Clark filled three of the next four places. With clutch support from Kenny Linville (12th), Steve Payne (14th), Tom Dycus (17th), and Mike Jenkins (21st), the Raging Red Line earned another hard-fought regional banner. Coach Fitch paid our men a nice compliment following the clash, observing, "The Daviess County runners get that determination on their faces and run even tougher when they get behind."

State Meet '83

We did not have the front runners to make a realistic charge for the top spot at the state finals. Regardless, our young men put forth a very credible effort. Led by Roberts (13th), Dechman (23rd) and Clark (25th), the Panthers achieved a top three finish for the tenth time in 14 years.

Tradition is a weapon that you can't really see, smell or touch, but I guarantee you it is something athletes can feel; it is grown through seeds of physical exertion and consistent results. The '83 gang certainly added another solid chapter to the growing Daviess County legacy of excellence.

— 1984 —

Respect

In '84, we had the most interesting mix possible on our sixteen man squad. Six experienced seniors greeted a sophomore and nine energetic freshmen that had more than a touch of collective mischievousness. One would think the youngsters would, either by nature, or through intimidation, be inclined to show a certain amount of respect toward their veteran teammates. Not this bunch! The rookies knew how to use their strength in numbers and thrived on aggravating the fire out of the seniors.

Our team captains were Bill Dechman and Tom Dycus. Both were very passionate about the sport and our program and did a great job of leading, both verbally and with their daily practice habits. One afternoon Tom was assigned the risky task of leading the ninth graders through a distance workout, circling the perimeter of Hillcrest Golf Course several times. At some point during the run, the freshmen decided they had all of Tom's chiding leadership that they were willing to take. Passing along the top of a cement wall that held back water about nine feet deep, they ganged up on their captain and dragged him toward the lake. Tom recalled, "I was shocked. Some of them had really taken up with me as their buddy, but I couldn't fight them off. They almost ripped my clothes off (getting me to the water). Then . . . kerplunk . . . splash! They threw me in shoes and all. I got out hollering 'ya'll are gonna pay for this!' By that time they had about 200 yards on me. All I could do was sit on the wall - so mad I could spit bullets - with lake moss hanging all over me." Nothing like respect!

A couple of our older guys got a late start in their training, so I held them out of the first three meets, therefore we were a bit shorthanded when the season opened at the St. Xavier Invitational. As usual, St. X and Trinity came out with "both guns a-blazing," finishing one-two. Louisville Southern was third, and we tied region foe Madisonville through five men, but they beat us in the tiebreaker (sixth man). Bill Dechman initiated his senior year with a fifth place run (16:22) and a surprising three second advantage over Austin Dean, considered the top returnee in Western Kentucky. The next time we saw Madisonville, in late September, Dean dominated, but we bested his team 57–71, winning our own invitational.

Seven of our nine freshmen had never run a cross country meet prior to the '84 campaign. Through mid-October, we kept the spunky rascals in the junior varsity division of our big meets where they gained valuable experience and confidence. With a shortage of depth in our upperclassmen, it was evident that two or three of our youngsters would have to step into the varsity picture. The first one we moved up was Paul Warrenfeltz, who came through like an ace, finishing as our sixth man, fifteenth overall, in a dominant team performance at the conference meet. Two weeks later I added freshmen Troy Adkins and Rodney Bivins to the varsity mix.

Regional

Daviess County hosted the regional at Hillcrest Golf Course where a large, raucous crowd expected to witness a real brawl between ourselves, North Hardin and Madisonville. The challenge loomed even larger for the Panthers than most folks realized. We had lost our #2 man, Dean Roberts, earlier in the week. Bragging rights for the top individual seemed to be a toss-up because Bill Dechman had once again turned back Austin Dean in their conference confrontation. Throwing Todd Henson, a well-coached but somewhat unheralded talent from Marshall County, into the mix gave this the look of a scintillating chase for the blue ribbon.

October 27th arose a beautiful day but one of cautious concern for runners accustomed to the cooler fall weather. As the men's teams lined up, the sun was brilliant, the wind whipping, and the temperature was near 80 degrees. When the race began, Austin Dean served notice that he meant business. Taking charge early, he galloped out to an ever-increasing gap over the field. By the time he hit the last 400 meter straightaway, Austin had built a commanding lead of around thirty seconds. On the final 150 meter decline leading to the chute, Austin's smooth gait wobbled. He quickly became disoriented, staggered several more yards and fell. The obvious and ugly reality of heat exhaustion was difficult to watch. Austin's coach yelled for him to get up and finish as Todd Henson stormed past . . . then two of our guys . . . one from Owensboro . . . one from North Hardin . . . another from North Hardin. By the time Austin was able to collapse across the line, he was in 26th place.

Anyone who has been around cross country for long has likely witnessed a similar scene. In our sport, hydration is often an issue and must absolutely be attended to, regardless of weather. Something that must be addressed is the coach or meet director's responsibility in a situation such as this. We need to evaluate our priorities when the spirit of competition and the health of our athletes collide! Is it worth the risk, for example, to let an overheated athlete finish, even if there are just a few yards left?

Fortunately, Austin Dean recovered and his team finished third, advancing to State with 86 points. North Hardin put together an excellent effort with six in the top nineteen and 55 points. There were, how-ever, five red jerseys near the front filled with Bill Dechman, Steve Payne, Tom Dycus, Paul Warrenfeltz, and Kenny Linville. Our guys showed great determination in overcoming the impact of Robert's absence on the course, and our 40 points was very sufficient reason for celebration.

State Meet '84

We were still shorthanded when we arrived in Lexington the first weekend of November, but I knew our men would represent the school well. Leading the Panther charge were team captains Bill Dechman, coming home eighteenth, and Tom Dycus, who had perhaps his best performance of the year (29th). Obviously, the forced cross-training in the lake during the summer paid big dividends for Tom! Payne (31st) and Linville (51st) were next. Freshman Paul Warrenfeltz completed our scoring, and fellow rookies Troy Adkins and Rodney Bivins responded to the stress of their first state meet by racing to personal best times. Results tallied, we wrapped up the season in fourth place.

The lighthearted younger portion of our squad had made great strides as the season progressed. Nonetheless, with no seniors returning for '85, two questions came to mind. First, who would step into a leadership position? Secondly, if a new captain did emerge would he too experience mutiny on the bounty and have to walk the gangplank?

— 1985 —

Painting for the Stuarts

Artie Marx taught elementary physical education in our school sys-tem for 29 years, which pretty well qualifies him for sainthood! A New York City transplant, Artie was quite a personality who knew more corny jokes than you could shake a stick at. The kids loved him! Artie handled the cross country coaching duties at Daviess County Middle School and developed a nice feeder system for our program.

For a couple of summers in the mid 80's Artie and I painted houses. We lined up one job to paint for George and Carolyn Stuart. You must understand that coaches are continually sizing up potential athletes and coming up with angles on how to get them out for the team. I had gotten to know Mark Stuart a bit while teaching at the middle school and tried unsuccessfully to recruit him as he moved to the high school his freshman year. The next summer, when Artie and I lined up the painting job for Mark's parents, I came up with a scheme. Mark was quite a cerebral young man with a mannerly "still waters run deep" type of personality. Of course, I just wanted "still waters" to run! I knew Mark enjoyed the analytical challenges that math classes offered, and each year I put together a season summary chocked full of times, numbers, and stats. I armed myself with three different booklets as we headed for the Stuart's to paint. My first order of business was to say hello to Mark and hand him the summaries. I asked him to read them, but I knew he would digest them. In spite of the fact that Artie spilled a gallon of paint on the Stuart's back deck that first day, we gave them a decent paint job, and Mark Stuart was on hand when practice began a few weeks later. Mission accomplished!

Youth Movement—What Pressure?

Mark became a part of what might have been the youngest and most fun-loving (those two qualities seem to go hand in hand) team that I have ever coached. That year ('85) our top seven would consist of a freshman, Steve Gilbert; five sophomores: Stuart, Paul Warrenfeltz, Rodney Bivins, Jimmy Vanover and Troy Adkins; and a junior Swedish exchange student, Gustaf Mark. Gustaf was a pleasant, engaging young man with a soccer and orienteering background, but no cross country experience. Gustaf was also a very truthful fellow as one of our local sportswriters, Brian Rickard, found out. Midway through the season Brian interviewed Gustaf for a feature story and asked him about the difference between Americans and Swedes. Gustaf's painfully blunt reply . . ."a lot of people are more fat here . . . junk food, definitely!"

The newspaper always does a nice season preview on the area teams. We had graduated six seniors from the '84 squad that finished fourth at state, and with no seniors on this squad I didn't see the need of putting unnecessary anxiety on our very inexperienced youngsters. County rival Apollo, on the other hand, was a veteran group with a number of seniors and had very high expectations. I decided to deflect the pressure on them and flat out stated to reporter Rich Suwanski, "Apollo is the team to beat." I suppose that was a bit sneaky because our practices and time trials revealed the potential for a terrific season.

Our first meet was a quadrangular with the local teams. Our guys went out hard the first mile, but our youthful inexperience was exposed, and at the halfway mark Apollo had come back and raced ahead of us. Surprisingly, our young team that was nearly as "green" as it was red matured by leaps and bounds the next mile and a half; the final tally showed us with 29 points. Second place Apollo had 46. We followed that meet with several strong performances, including invitational wins at Marshall County, Owensboro, and our own Classic.

Gustaf Mark (1.) and Paul Warrenfeltz race down
a hill at Hillcrest Golf Course in 1985.

I had scheduled a special trip for the first weekend of October and knew that the Vulcan Classic in Birmingham, Alabama would probably bring us back down to earth. Nevertheless, I have always been convinced that if you want to be the best, you have to run against the best. This meet, in its infancy, would later become one of the earliest recognized national caliber meets. It was already a strong Southern competition with teams from Alabama, Georgia, and Tennessee among those present. The race was very hotly contested among the top squads. Riverdale, Georgia finished with 97 points, just two less than Huntsville, Alabama's 99. Grissom, Alabama had 105 but the surprise winner . . . Daviess County, Kentucky, with 91 points! Our kids were growing up.

By the regional, our youngsters were battle tested and ready to go. When the dust settled in the ten team meet, we had tallied 39 points, beating second place Apollo by 45. Three fairly inexperienced young men led us to victory. Gustaf Mark came in second overall (16:48), Paul Warrenfeltz third (16:51), and Mark Stuart fourth (17:07), over the tough 5,000 meters of Hillcrest Golf Course.

At state the following week in Lexington, Warrenfeltz capped off his fine season with a 15th place finish, Stuart 22nd, and Mark 29th, leading the team to a commendable third place. The best way to describe the '85 season . . . pure fun!

Oh, by the way . . . I would have painted the Stuart's house the previous summer for nothing!

— 1986 —

Born Runner

August is a great month; both Pam and I celebrate our birthdays, the sun shines brightly on my old Kentucky home, and cross country practice is in full swing. August 12th of '86 saw our family receive a gift that made the month even more special. After several hours of painful labor, Pam gave birth to our second son, Matt. I knew that if we had just three more we would have enough for a scoring team. However, I wisely resisted sharing that thought with Pam for awhile! Time passes so quickly, and this bouncing baby boy would one day also make his presence known in a Daviess County jersey. For the time being, however, we would just have to concentrate on things like Matt taking his first step.

Where Have All the Seniors Gone?

Like the previous year, the 1986 team was very young. As a matter of fact, we had no seniors on the squad. A couple of the guys we were counting on chose not to run. With only ten guys on the team, depth was a problem. Interestingly, when school began, we picked up a Swedish exchange student for the second year in a row, Paul Tedenby. Paul was a handsome, well built young man who loved to look at himself in the mirror and was thrilled with the selection of young ladies in America. He quickly picked up the team "Romeo" label, and though he was behind conditioning-wise, Paul's fitness improved rapidly once he began to train with us.

Mark Stuart had made tremendous strides through his first year of running and opened the '86 season with a solid win in the City-County Meet, on a warm and humid Tuesday afternoon. Four days later Mark stamped himself as one of Kentucky's elite runners, touring the 3.05 mile layout at Marshall County in 15:45. Mark had a terrific sense of pace and like many good runners, Mark didn't necessarily pick up the tempo during a race; he simply did not slow down. Mark also was a terrific hill runner. Far too many young runners either slow down as they approach a hill or speed up as they climb and die at the top. I try to teach my runners not to attack a hill but rather to "keep the rhythm of your race." The stride is naturally going to shorten as it meets the incline and the arms may swing a bit more aggressively, but concentration should be on maintaining the rate of effort. Mark was like a steady machine over a hilly layout!

The team had four invitational wins, as well as the conference and regional titles, going into the state meet. Our state squad consisted of juniors Stuart, Tedenby, Paul Warrenfeltz, Troy Adkins, and Richard Howard, and two sophomores, Steve Gilbert and Jon Locher. Stuart's breakout season included some nice wins and swift times, and we felt he was a legitimate threat to win the individual title in Lexington. Team-wise, Rich Rostel's senior-dominated Louisville Trinity bunch had been virtually untouchable. *Inside Track* magazine had them ranked #1 in the South. We were ranked #18 in Dixie and second in Kentucky. Trinity lived up to their billing with an incredible performance, placing six in the top ten and scoring 20 points. The only scene I had ever witnessed that came close was Daviess County's state meet effort in 1971.

With Trinity controlling this meet, the race was really for second place. Our young guys answered the call as Stuart finished 11th, Tedenby 15th, Warrenfeltz 22nd, Gilbert 29th, and Adkins 68th. Our team score of 115 edged out Louisville Holy Cross by nine points for the runner-up trophy. We were a bit disappointed for Mark Stuart, but he seemed to be a bit under the weather. Little did we know the real depth of Mark's effort. It was substantiated when he went to the doctor a couple of days later. The doctor was surprised Mark had even finished the race, much less finished eleventh. Mark had double pneumonia!

Mark Stuart (#261) followed closely by Paul Tedenby
(#262) near the mile mark of the 1986 state meet.

— 1987 —

Claycomb

In the fall of '87, Mike Claycomb came in as a freshman. Mike was one of those unforgettable kids destined to make an impact on the team one way or another. Something in his body could produce more energy than the Hoover Dam. I had known Mike for a number of years, having been his physical education teacher at Maceo Elementary School. Later, he would tell me that I was the one who gave him his first spanking. Indeed . . . Mike was in the second grade. The best I recall we were working on a tumbling unit, and one of the stations was a balance beam about 18" high. Safety was my main concern, and I warned the kids not to try anything dangerous. Those words probably had not even risen to the rafters before Mike did a back flip off of the beam. Although I was impressed by his gymnastic ability, I had to take the little stinker to the office and give him a swat.

I loved Mike's passion for life. He was absolutely going to get the most out of every day, and with him any given moment could explode into an adventure! All the extra activity certainly kept Mike fit. We might be on a seven mile run, but by the time he took side trips to chase a rabbit, pet a dog, do a few back flips (which he had now perfected), or do any of about a thousand other things that could distract him, Mike probably stretched the distance to about ten miles.

Mike lived way out near the county line, over 20 miles from the high school. When we started 7 a.m. summer practice Mike's freshman year, his dad would drop him off at my house on his way to work, and Mike would ride in with me. He always got to my house about 6 a.m. and waited outside for me to wake up and get ready. One morning Pam and I woke to the melody of a strange "bird." She went to the front door and looked up to see Mike near the top of a tree in our front yard singing to the top of his lungs. From what I heard of the conversation, there was a distinct possibility that this early bird was about to get more than a worm!

Later in the season, on a recovery run, Mike found a dead squirrel. He carried that thing, dangling by its tail, for about six miles. He would sprint over to a tree and play like the squirrel was climbing, pretend it was talking, make it do "hand" gestures, and all sorts of other goofy things. I think the squirrel would really have liked Mike. The other guys on the team just laughed and shook their heads.

Mike did show the potential for being a pretty good cross country runner when we could keep him healthy. Over the next four years, Mike would have several impact races for us, but would also miss many important competitions because of concussions, broken bones, and such. In the spring of his freshman year, Mike discovered an event that would fit his personality perfectly . . . the pole vault.

The '87 campaign brought modest success with team victories in the City-County meet, the Owensboro Invitational, and the Big Eight Conference Championships. Several fellows impacted our scoring, including: seniors Troy Adkins, Richard Howard, and Chris Goodman; juniors Robert Murley and Jon Locher; and talented freshmen Mike Claycomb, Bob Foster, and Neal Anderson. Neal was physically mature for a ninth grader. His favorite exercise was overhand pull-ups, and he could hammer through about twenty-five of them. Neal's strength and work ethic resulted in his elevation to a consistent #2 position for us.

Our leader, however, as he had been in '86, was Mark Stuart. Mark had very few equals on the trails and rolled through most meets. The one guy who gave him fits seemed to be Carl Dillard of Christian County. Their duals were fun to watch, but usually wound up with Carl pulling away in the last 600 or so yards of the race. Mark couldn't quite solve the puzzle.

In the Halloween Day regional, on our home course, the team came up short of victory, but with a third place run we advanced to state. Dillard once again got the better of Stuart in the chase for the blue ribbon, winning the individual title for the third straight year.

Robert Murley sprints to the finish just ahead of
Richard Howard in the 1987 regional.

State Meet '87

There were several young men that seemed capable of crossing the finish stripe first in the '87 State Meet. Under a bright blue sky and a great day for a cross country race, Damian Nally of Lexington Lafayette took up the pacesetting chores with a very snappy first mile. Just beyond that point, Mark Stuart and his friendly rival, Carl Dillard, made it a trio at the front.

Stuart's steady pacing approach was just what the doctor ordered over the challenging terrain of the Steeplechase circles, as he hit nearly even splits of 4:56 (mile) and 10:02 (2 miles). Nally dropped first and the steady grind was finally more punishment than Dillard could take. Mark found himself alone on the last half mile of the course. As he made a final left hand turn, there was nothing but 200 yards of green grass and screaming spectators between Mark and the finish banner. Nally, however, had sneaked back up to within 20 or 25 yards, and I happened to be at that point to watch the fireworks. Mark had no idea Nally was back in contention. As he passed, I hollered, "He's 20 yards back, you gotta go!" In the noise and excitement, Mark thought I said, "Wait about 20 yards and go!" Nally had Mark measured and dashed by him about 100 yards from glory. Mark dug in and caught back up, but was out-legged in the final few strides, finishing a valiant effort as state runner-up.

Naturally, I felt bad for Mark, but he reacted from a very mature perspective that is so admirable in truly great athletes. There are far too many poor sports surrounding athletics, often in the form of frustrated fans or athletes who did not lay it all on the line. For Mark Stuart there was no agony of defeat. He had poured every ounce of grit he possessed into the challenge.

Mark recalled his emotions: "After the race I was completely, totally satisfied with my performance and had almost no disappointment. My attitude was basically, 'can you believe that finish?' For some reason the loss didn't bother me . . . I knew I had put everything I had out there." Indeed, that's the way it should be. I recall watching some of the great heavyweight boxing matches between men like Muhammad Ali and Joe Frazier. There was always lots of chatter leading up to the fight, but at the end of fifteen rounds, the talk was usually in the form of compliments and respect between the gallant competitors. We don't always walk away from the field of competition with the first place trophy, but it is extremely important that we leave as winners!

Neal Anderson completed his rookie high school season with a fine effort, 40th place. Newcomer Robert Murley was 58th, Richard Howard 71st, and Jon Locher 80th as the Panthers came back to Western Kentucky in eighth place.

Why is it that on the day when motivation and excitement is at its peak, the season has to end? We only had nine months to wait until the starter's pistol would signal the start of another campaign!

— 1988 —

The '88 rendition of Daviess County cross country mirrored the '85 team in many ways. We had a pleasant, hard-working group of kids who were fun to coach. The development of our strong sophomore class and production from the few seniors on the squad would prove to be critical to our success. One "ace in the hole" was Bob Foster. Bob had run some nice races as a freshman the previous year but came down with pneumonia just before the regional, ending his season. Healthy again, Bob looked great in pre-season training. Still, I was somewhat surprised when he burst into the lead just past the two mile point in our season-opener at the Marshall County Invitational and whipped many of Western Kentucky's premier harriers, winning on a muddy, wet course, in 17:00. Ten seconds later, fellow sophomore Neal Anderson finished fourth. The twosome traded off our #1 position from week to week, and at end of September our only loss was at the Tennessee Classic where Parkview, Georgia topped us 95–107. The challenging Vulcan Classic initiated the second half of the fall. Although we came back to Kentucky with the third place trophy, I was very pleased with the southern venture. Our results over a fairly harsh three mile terrain were: Neal Anderson (16:01), Bob Foster (16:05), Robert Murley (16:24), Steve Gilbert (16:35), Mike Claycomb (16:40), Mike Bruner (16:57), and Brian Clark (17:20).

Back at home a week later in our own Classic, Gordon Bocock's always hard-charging Pulaski County seven put the state picture in perspective with a stout 48 point total, well ahead of our 107. The very next meet we made the three hour trek east to Somerset for Pulaski County's invitational, perhaps the toughest regular season get-together in Kentucky. Coach Bocock always put on a fantastic meet.

Pulaski County only had football since the early 80's; therefore, their cross country numbers were always tremendous. Gordon transformed the weekend into a folksy extravaganza, complete with 3- to 4-feet tall team trophies and a cross country queen that they crowned at the meet. Teams across the state loved being a part of the festivities.

The good host intentions ended at the starting line. When the thirty-one visiting teams were sent home, the Maroons still had the gold trophy. The top four team scores read: Pulaski County 93, Louisville Trinity 96, Oldham County 153 and Daviess County 169.

Bob's Regional Surprise

The regional meet was hosted by Christian County High School, on the flat grounds of Hopkinsville Community College, making it seem like a track meet on grass. No team in the region had beaten us, and I expected a very stout performance from our crew, despite the fact that we were holding out one of our scorers in a disciplinary issue. The individual title was up for grabs, and I hoped that one of our guys would take the bull by the horns somewhere after the first mile or so. On a very chilly day, our guys heated up the trail with a determined effort, making up for their missing comrade. Warren Central's Kenny Chandler led the field through the first half of the skirmish. The Panther trio of Foster, Anderson, and Murley were part of a chase pack lurking just behind. Bob Foster was the first to negate the gap. As he passed Chandler, Bob not only took the lead, he took control! Running with the confidence of a veteran, Bob never looked back, stretching his lead to about 100 meters and winning impressively in 16:19. Rock-solid Neal Anderson was third (16:40) and reliable senior Robert Murley fifth (16:45). Two more sophomores closed out our scoring with Mike Claycomb 14th (17:21) and Mike Bruner 15th (17:21). Senior Chris Goodman came through big-time with a personal best time by a whopping 55 seconds (17:23).

The events of the day certainly were a confidence builder, but the big boys would be waiting in the Bluegrass.

State Meet '88

Going into the premier event of the year, I felt like our top four men were about equal to co-favorites Pulaski County and Trinity. Both had taken us to the proverbial woodshed two weeks earlier, but we still had ideas about making it a three team tussle.

The day broke cool and windy, and several competitors wore light gloves and undershirts to help fight off the chill. Usually, once the clash begins, adrenaline neutralizes any weather concerns. Many distance runners prefer somewhat chilly temperatures, and I have seen some superfast performances in the cold.

The race was worth the price of the ticket! Lafayette's Damian Nally, the individual defender, took the pace out tough and made it two straight titles, but the team race was where the fire was popping. It was one of those deals where no one was sure of the outcome just from watching the race. Follow closely here. Pulaski County placed four men in front of our third. Our fourth man crossed two spots before Trinity's fourth and our fifth was 15 positions ahead of Pulaski's fifth, but 14 behind Trinity's. Indeed, twelve of the top 24 competitors in the chute at 5,000 meters were from these three schools. Bob Foster came through with another gritty effort for the Panthers, placing sixth. He was followed by Neal Anderson (17th), Steve Gilbert (18th), Robert Murley (22nd), and Mike Bruner (42nd). Our team score of 99 was good for third place, behind Trinity's 83 and Pulaski County's 88. We had run perhaps our best race of the year in the pressure cooker of the state meet. I could not have asked for more!

— 1989 —

The '89 season saw a mixture of veterans and several very young runners in our lineup. Neal Anderson had moved to Paducah, but Bob Foster was coming off of a super sophomore year, looking to repeat as individual regional titlist and improve on his sixth place finish at state. Bob certainly had some talent; however, his work ethic was what set him apart from the crowd. Bob lived far out in the county and did not always have others to train with in the critical summer months. Bob would faithfully "lace 'em up" and crank out 70, 80, and occasionally 100 mile weeks in preparation for the season. We had a very promising freshman class that included Jason Clark, Chris Wells, Eric Massie, and Jeramy Kazlauskas (Kaz). Going into the season, I would not have dreamed that we would be counting on three of those freshmen among our seven varsity runners at the end of the year.

"Left in the Regional Dust"

Late in the fall we hosted the regional. Our home course had been relocated from Hillcrest Golf Course to a large area behind Owensboro Community College that had been a cornfield just a year or two earlier. The footing was still a bit rough, and the turf seemed to be as much dirt and dust as it was grass. Warren Central, led by senior Kenny Chandler, established themselves as favorites to win their first regional championship in what looked to be a close team battle.

Although a bit apprehensive, I felt that rookies Clark, Massie, and Wells had earned themselves a varsity spot. They were going to have to come up big for us. Junior Mike Claycomb, our solid and dependable second man all fall, came up very ill just days before the meet. Still, we sent Mike and the three freshmen to the starting line along with juniors Bob Foster and Mike Bruner and sophomore Brian Clark. The seventh man position on our team had been a tough choice, and I went with Wells over Kazlauskas. Interestingly, Kaz would eventually become a state individual champion and our first national finalist.

It was an uncharacteristically warm and sunny late October day. The top four teams would advance to the state meet. The race pretty much went as expected for the first two miles with Bob Foster, Kenny Chandler, and Apollo's Kevin Schwartz battling up front and a great team race underway. Although Warren Central was ahead of us, it looked as if we would advance to state. However, the wheels fell off over the hills of the last mile. Bob, suffering from asthma, became victim to the change of weather, pollen, and dust; he fell through the pack to a 17th place finish. It seemed that our young guys panicked when they saw their leader going "out the back door" and some followed suit. The result was a very hard to swallow fifth place finish for the team, and we failed to advance to state. Four of our guys did qualify as individuals, including Bob, but for us it has always been about the team. To add insult to injury the headline in our local newspaper the next day read, "DCHS Left in Regional Dust." We had won six of the previous seven regional titles. I suppose the headline was part of the price you pay for success. However, I really felt like the focus should have been on achievements of the teams who beat us. All we could do was learn from the disappointment and look toward '90. To his credit, Bob rebounded in the cool weather one week later to finish third in the state meet, only 11 seconds behind the champion.

V

— A Special Decade–The 90's —

— 1990 —

The "Dust Crew"

To be knocked down is one thing, but to stay on the canvas is another. For several months the failure to advance to the '89 state meet had bugged me, and I couldn't wait to start practice in the summer of '90. I didn't want to throw the disappointment of the previous year in the face of our guys, but I didn't want them to forget either. I decided to take the aggravating headline in our town newspaper after the '89 regional and use it to our advantage. I purchased several caps and had the words "Dust Crew" printed on the front. It served as a not-so-subtle reminder that we had a mission to accomplish.

Our in-county rival, Apollo, led by junior Kevin Schwartz, had perhaps their strongest team ever coming back, and the season began with the Eagles besting us by ten points at the Fort Campbell Invitational. Our two teams ran neck and neck throughout the fall as did Bob Foster and Schwartz. One of the really pleasant surprises for us was the development of sophomore Jeramy Kazlauskas. Jeramy had not been in the varsity lineup in '89 and was only our #4 freshman on that team. What a difference a year had made! Jeramy started showing some real potential as a cross country runner and worked himself into our #2 spot, behind Foster. Kaz unfortunately developed a nagging hip injury in late season, and we sat him out of the Christian County Invitational, hoping he'd be ready to go when it counted most. Without him, Apollo beat us 82 to 95.

Jeramy did toe the line at the regional championships a week later, but could not overcome his injury enough to be a factor. His presence, however, seemed to boost the team confidence, and our other six men took up the slack. Foster, as usual, was solid with a second place effort. The surprise of the day was freshman Steve Bair, who stepped up big time, running a personal best 17:17 and finishing 11th. Sophomore Jason Clark (12th), junior Mark Lattin (14th), and sophomore Mark O'Bryan (17th) quickly closed our scoring. Our guys averaged 21 seconds faster per man than on the same course where we had competed the previous week. The result was a very satisfying 56 to 66 cushion over runner-up Apollo. The "Dust Crew" had completed our goal of regaining the regional team title and advancing to state.

Regional would be Kazlauskas' last race of the season; he just could not get over the hip injury. Without Jeramy, we were not quite up to par at the Kentucky Horse Park and finished sixth. Bob Foster culminated his outstanding high school career with another third place effort on the rolling bluegrass hills. He would take his talents to Southern Illinois University the next year, joining former DC star Mark Stuart. Ironically, versatile senior Mike Claycomb, who had to sit out the '90 season while recovering from a summer pole vaulting accident, also signed with SIU where he had an outstanding career as a vaulter and decathlete.

Bob Foster was named to the Kentucky All-State Team three consecutive years during his career at Daviess County High School.

— 1991 —

What about God?

In a society that seemingly is distancing itself from our Creator more and more, athletics is often the refreshing exception. It is great to see teams continue to huddle for pre-competition prayer, to see athletes point to the sky acknowledging their source of strength, and to see them kneel with their opponents after the skirmish, offering thanks for the blessing of sport. Lots of folks object to this type behavior, saying it's showy or insincere, even unconstitutional. They will look for faults these athletes may have (as if any of us are perfect) and call them hypocrites. Hmmm! I will take my chances anytime with a group that will be in a hotel room 200 miles from home, on a Friday night before a meet, having a time of Scripture study and devotion. That was a common practice for our guys.

The '91 "edition of tradition" was very mature and good natured, just a super bunch of young men. Leadership was not an issue because so many of them exemplified the discipline a coach longs to see in his athletes. Much of this stemmed from faith-based principles they lived out everyday. People noticed. As a matter of fact, our local newspaper ran a great article entitled "Religion & Sports" that featured our squad. They asked different runners how their Christian beliefs affected their performance. Junior Jason Clark, who was already a licensed minister as a member of Maceo Baptist Church, responded, "To me, God is a focal point, and my faith allows me to stay focused on running and who I'm doing it for . . . He gives me strength and courage to run and to do it for Him." Senior Mark Lattin, who was a vice-president of our school's Fellowship of Christian Athletes huddle, concurred, "He (God) gives me the gift (to run) . . . it's up to me to do everything I can to give the glory back to Him."

As a coach, I try to allow . . . even create . . . an environment where young men feel free to express themselves and grow in their relationship with God. Yes, I know we are a public school, but I also know that the principles that this nation was founded on are the same ones that will give young athletes the moral foundation and fiber necessary to become men that will lead our country's quest for continued greatness . . . and I will go to bat for that cause anytime!

Obeying the biblical advice that "faith and works go together," our guys were certainly willing to sweat. Junior Jeremy Kruger was the perfect example of the blue collar attitude they possessed. Jeremy's granddad owned a farm out in the western part of Daviess County where Jeremy raised his own tobacco patch. After morning practices in July and August, Jeremy spent many hot and humid summer days in the fields. Still, he only missed one practice in four years of high school running. Talk about discipline!

"notyeP divaD"

As a coach, it is often the incidents and personalities (with their quirks) that I recall most vividly about past seasons. When I think about it, that's the way it should be, enjoying the athletes!

I talked senior David Peyton into coming out for cross country. David was a bright young man who had some major reservations about the adjective "distance" in front of the noun "runner." David thought the 800 meter run on the track the previous spring was quite a tour of endurance, but somehow couldn't say no to my invitation to hit the cross country trails. David had a unique talent. He could read backward as quickly as he could forward, pronouncing the syllables with an eloquence that completely baffled me. For instance, the phrase "it's raining outside," became, "edistuo gniniar s'ti." David could read page after page like that, not missing a beat! His upbeat personality added a lot of light moments to the daily grind.

Going into the regional, junior Jeramy Kazlauskas had quietly pieced together a very solid campaign. In the eleven meets up to that point, he had won only two races, one of which was a dual meet, but had been in the top five spots in all of them. The team followed a similar script, winning five small meets but finishing no worst than fourth, including some major invitationals.

We always enjoyed running on the Marshall County High School campus in the lakes area of Western Kentucky, and it seemed we always competed well there. Our #2 man, Jason Clark, was hospitalized with severe stomach pains on Wednesday. However, there he was three days later, lined up with his teammates, ready to defend the regional title.

To the man, our scorers showed a determined toughness, resulting in our best team effort of the season. Sophomore Steve Bair hit the line in 5th place, Lattin 8th, Kruger 9th, and Clark 14th. Kazlauskas, however, was the man! Taking the lead at 1½ miles, Kaz scorched the last half of the course, blasting out to a 34 second win and busting Bob Foster's course record with a time of 16:11.

The victory was nice, but we packed our bags for Lexington knowing the challenge would be severe. Top ranked Louisville Trinity had dominated the field at the October 26th Meet of Champions, scoring

33 points. St. Xavier edged our team 94–97 for second, and both were ranked ahead of us. Johnny Baum of Louisville Holy Cross was projected as the overwhelming favorite for the individual crown, having already run a 15:05 (3 miles) on the new course in the campground area of the Kentucky Horse Park that would serve as the state meet site.

State Meet '91

Baum was all business after the pistol sounded; however, he had five hounds nipping at his heels. Right in the middle of that group was Jeramy Kazlauskas. Baum held the contenders at bay, victorious in 15:28. Boone County's Eric Vanlaningham was second best (15:35), but the surprise of the day   had to be Kaz. Jeramy came through with a huge personal best (15:39), his third place leading our charge. We couldn't catch up to Trinity, but captured the silver with splendid performances from Bair (19th), Clark (22nd), Lattin (26th), and our linguistic specialist, Peyton (45th). As he might say, "rilem flah a rof dab ton" . . ."not bad for a half miler!"

So . . . was the collective devotion and integrity of this team sincere? I believe so! Allow me to follow-up on a few of the guys. Mark Lattin spent several years in the Lexington area after college, serving in faith-based ministry to students at the University of Kentucky. Jeremy Kruger worked his way through college and graduate school and opened a clinic in Lexington as a physical therapist. Jason Clark now pastors the Salvisa Baptist Church in Harrodsburg, Kentucky. By the way, Jason does most of his running these days trying to keep up with his five children (enough for a team score), including . . . are you ready for this . . . quadruplets! The point being the principles that young people form during their critical teen-age years tend to stay with them. Most still have the same personal morals and habits 10 and 20 years later; as a coach, I have to understand that there is a much larger issue here than just running!

— 1992 —

Out of the Smoking Area

As expected, our '92 team was led by senior Jeramy Kazlauskas, a very personable young man who had the heart of a lion. Jeramy was in my weights class during that fall semester. In mid-September, I took the class to the track for a mile run. Jeramy cruised through, running an easy 5:55. We had a sophomore in the class named Charlie Moore who stayed right with Jeramy, running 5:56.   When they finished I approached Charlie and stated, "Charlie, you ought to be running cross country."

"I'd like that," he said. At that time, our school had a smoking area for students, which we got rid of a couple of years later. I asked Charlie if he smoked.

"Yeah, but I've been looking for a reason to stop!" I told Charlie that if he ran he couldn't smoke or even go into the smoking area.

Charlie said, "You mean I couldn't even go in there to talk to my friends?"

"Nope, and you'd also have to get a physical." I figured that to be the end of the conversation.

About three days later Charlie came to me and said, "Here's my physical!" We were half way through the season, and I was a bit surprised. I did not normally let people join the team so late; however, I was the one who started this. I asked Charlie if he had quit smoking, and he assured me he had, so I hesitantly let him join the team.

One week after Charlie joined us, we competed against the majority of the state's best teams in the Franklin County Invitational at the Kentucky Horse Park. We averaged 16:57 and finished second as a team; however, Louisville Trinity cleaned our clock, 37–110. Three weeks later, on the same course at the Meet of Champions, our average time was actually one second slower and both Trinity and St. Xavier gave us a thrashing.

We went into the regional on our tough home course certainly in need of some breakthroughs, and several Panthers responded. Jeramy Kazlauskas had a stellar performance, touring the challenging layout in a course record of 16:14. Junior Steve Bair continued his steady season with a fifth place effort. The improvement of Charlie Moore (9th) suddenly made us a much better squad, and senior leaders Jason Clark (14th) and Jeremy Kruger (19th) ensured our eleventh conquest of the region over a span of 15 years.

State Meet '92

Although our regional effort was very good, state was much better. Despite the fact that Jeramy Kazlauskas had been beaten at the Horse Park by St. Xavier's John Perkins two weeks earlier, we felt he had a great shot at coming home as the individual champ. Kaz had eight wins to his credit during the fall and was intent on completing the season in a very special way. We came up with a strategy for him to bust a strong move up a hill just beyond the two mile mark and see if Perkins or anyone else was game. Lots of good runners have a plan, but champions carry it out! At the very spot we designated, Kaz executed his tactic to perfection. No one could cover his move as Kaz blasted through the last mile in 5:07 on his way to a rousing triumph, running 15:27 for three miles.   Kaz reflected, "Going through that tunnel of spectators the last 400 meters and realizing you are going to be the state champion is very emotional."

The finish chute at the state meet is quite involved. As he crossed the line, Kaz encountered what seemed to be an endless process of ropes tied to stakes. Spotting an equally emotional Cheri Kazlauskas a few yards away in the throng of onlookers, he took the short way out. Kaz hopped over the ropes, cleared the chute, and gave his mom a big championship hug.

Steve Bair also turned in an outstanding effort (7th-16:09). Our third man that day was Charlie Moore in 21st place (16:34) with Jason Clark right on his heels (22nd-16:37). It seemed to be a day where every Panther decided to step it up, and the biggest surprise may have been in our fifth position as freshman Derek Brown cut nearly 40 seconds off of his Meet of Champions time, gliding home in 16:52 and 30th place.

Louisville Trinity's senior-dominated bunch continued the excellence they displayed all year with a 36 point meet; however, our 67 points was the lowest state meet total of any Panther squad in 21 years, and we had much to celebrate with our runner-up feat.

Oh, by the way, Charlie Moore never went back to the smoking area!

Jeramy Kazlauskas crosses the finish line as the
individual state champion in 1992.

— 1993 —

Keep Your Drawers Up Steve

I have always enjoyed the varied personalities of each team member.
Steve Bair was one of those happy-go-lucky types who worked hard and
had enough speed to be a threat to win in a close race. One such race was
our '93 opener, the Marshall County Invitational. Steve and Jim Garnett
of Christian County had battled it out for three miles, and it was obvious that the kick in the last several meters would determine the winner.
I noticed, however, Steve tugging at his shorts late in the race. I couldn't
figure out what was going on but knew he was going to have to use both
arms to out-sprint Garnett. As they neared the finish line, Steve got up

on his toes, pumping his arms like crazy. With every stride his shorts dropped a bit lower. Undeterred, Steve gained a very slight lead and won by less than a second . . . with the waistband of his shorts closer to his knees than his hips. Thankfully, Steve had his "whitie tighties" on underneath. Unabashed, he simply pulled his shorts up and began to celebrate his win. Steve later asked me if we could give the video of his finish to the school news team to be broadcast. You have got to love a kid that can laugh at himself! We made sure Steve had shorts with a high-quality waistband for the remainder of the season.

Steve was our team leader and certainly had a great year, eventually earning honors on the Kentucky Super Team, but junior Charlie Moore's star was about to rise. The second race of the season, the Warren East Invitational, saw Steve get his second straight win, running 15:54, one second faster than Charlie. In the final twelve races of '93, Charlie would break the tape eight times. To Steve's credit, he never resented Charlie's success, making a great unspoken statement to our guys about the importance of the team.

Late in September our basketball coach, Al Walter, informed me that he had timed a Swedish exchange student in 5:26 for a mile in preseason conditioning. Remembering how well two other exchange students had fit in back in '85 and '86, and thinking back to Charlie Moore's situation a year earlier, I decided to track the young man down. Jon Eriksen was a very easy-going and engaging young man whose school back home in Sweden offered no athletics. Jon had a beautiful, fluid stride and was in remarkable aerobic fitness. Lightning was most likely not going to strike twice in the same place (Charlie had been an exception), but Jon's chances of making the basketball cut were very slim, and I allowed him to join our team. I figured it would be good for international relations if nothing else!

A Snowy Regional

One of the challenging aspects of athletics is the elements. Cross country season in Kentucky begins in very warm weather. One year we left from a Saturday morning invitational with an actual air temperature of 100 degrees. The Kentucky High School Athletic Association has since passed a rule that if the heat index (heat and humidity combination) is above 105 degrees no contests or practices can be conducted.

Such was not the case in the 1993 regional. The forecast in Hopkinsville, Kentucky was for some very premature winter-like weather. You're not going to win many cross country races in sweats and heavy clothing, so when days like this appear you just have to "cowboy up" and tough it out. I have learned through experience that if an athlete can keep his head and hands warm, then he can endure cold races very well. We decided to go with sock caps and the one size fits all cotton gloves that you can get at K-Mart or Wal-Mart for about a dollar a pair. Normally, half of the guys will buy white gloves and half red, then they trade one of each . . . a little cold weather tradition that has been passed on through the years.

On Friday evening, in our team meeting at the hotel, I knew I had to prepare the guys for what they were going to face the next day. The conditions would freak out some teams. If we would embrace the challenge, we could use the nasty weather to our advantage; besides, it would make the memories more special.

We woke up a few hours later, Halloween morning, to 26 degrees, a 15 to 20 mile an hour wind, and an inch of snow on the ground with the flakes still flying . . . sideways! The course on the grounds of Hopkinsville Community College was normally flat and fast, but it was apparent that the slippery turf and 10 degree wind chill factor was going to slow the times down significantly.

We always encourage the guys to be sweating when they go to the starting line, and on this day, I'm sure none of them were. Still, we completed a vigorous warm-up and were ready when the starter's pistol was fired. When the wind was at the runners' backs or coming in from the side, it was bearable. When it came in head on, the chill created was dangerous. Charlie Moore did what had become his habit by now. Going to the front and attacking the race, he won in 16:11. The other guys also took it up a notch as dependable Steve Bair placed third, surprising Jon Eriksen fifth (I suppose lightning can strike twice!), and sophomore Derek Brown seventh. Junior Eurel Maddox, running perhaps his best race of the year, closed out our scoring in tenth place. I was very excited for Eurel because he was fighting a tough battle at home. His father's health was not good, and Eurel desperately wanted to perform well for him. Our 16:59 average and 26 points was a super effort in the adverse conditions. By the end of the day, I was hoping for snow a week later!

The 1993 squad dashes off the starting line in a
cold and snowy regional championship.

'93 State Championship

A couple of days before we left for state, Eurel Maddox came and asked me if his dad could ride up with us to Lexington. In those days I drove the bus, so we called Mr. Maddox a chaperone, and he spent an enjoyable trip with us.

As was our normal habit, we arrived at the Horse Park about an hour before dark on Friday to jog the course and review our strategy for the next morning. I am a huge believer in the importance of the team in every scenario surrounding the state meet. It's very easy to let the pressure of the event have a negative effect on performance. Being with your "brothers" seems to act as a safety net and helps calm the jitters as the race approaches. On this particular evening, David Clark, a senior who focused on the 400 meters during track season, asked me if he could skip the team run and prepare by running the course alone. It was an unusual request, but David assured me he could best prepare mentally in an isolated situation. Somewhat hesitantly, I relented. As the rest of the team jogged the course discussing how we wanted to run each section, I would see David on a different part, stopped and glaring at that portion of the layout. He did this over every section of the course. I suppose converted quarter-milers have a different mindset!

The weather had remained chilly, but not near as nasty as one week before. At race time it was 35 degrees and spitting snow. We came into the meet as co-favorites with Louisville Trinity. Two weeks prior, at the Meet of Champions, our two teams had actually tied, and Trinity beat us by going to the tiebreaker (first #6 man to finish).

The race for the individual title was never in doubt. Charlie Moore's amazing odyssey from the smoking area one year earlier continued. Now the only thing he was smoking was his competition. Charlie hit the mile mark in a smooth 5:00 and sailed through 2 miles in 10:10. Breaking away from the field, he cruised to victory in a swift 15:27 over the three mile course. Charlie's first priority after entering the finish chute was to search the steady stream of runners behind him for teammates. He was ecstatic when he saw Steve Bair finishing a solid career in fifth place. After that we had a four man pack between 16:39 and 16:49: Brown (26th), Eriksen (27th), freshman Chris Lanham (31st), and Clark (32nd). In the final tally we earned an exciting team championship, winning by 17 points over second place Louisville St. Xavier and 39 points better than Trinity. What a feeling!

Eurel Maddox struggled a bit, finishing as our seventh man in a still respectable 64th place. He was somewhat disappointed, but his dad was very proud of him and seemed to relish the opportunity to witness and share in Eurel's effort and the championship the team had garnered.

A few months later, at about 9:30 on a Thursday evening, the phone rang at home. It was Eurel. His father had just passed away, and Eurel wanted me to come to his home. I was able to see the family and pay my respects to Mr. Maddox even before the coroner arrived. Looking back, I am sure that Mr. Maddox' chaperoning our state meet was God-appointed and something that Eurel will always hold close to his heart. I will too.

— 1994 —

Most boys in the Bluegrass State have dreams of growing up and playing basketball for the Big Blue. You have to be a Kentuckian to understand it. When the Wildcats are on television, the roads are empty, the stores aren't doing much business, and there ain't a whole lot of work going on. The mental health and well-being of lots of folks in our fine commonwealth is contingent upon the outcome of University of Kentucky basketball games.

Although the fact is hidden from many kids and their well-meaning parents, not everyone is cut out to be a basketball star. Don't get me wrong, basketball is a great game. However, I have seen lots of kids put all their energy and time into the sport only to get to their junior or senior year and gather splinters sitting on the bench, wishing they had kept open some other athletic avenues.

In track season of '94, we gained one of those frustrated young men. Josh Skillman, an extremely hard worker and one of the finest individuals I have ever coached, began training with our distance team. He loved it and decided to concentrate solely on running as a senior. Charlie Moore, Chris Lanham, and Derek Brown all returned with state meet experience, and I felt that our continuing goal of a top three finish was well within reach.

As we rolled into the season, Josh Skillman quickly adjusted to the hills and trails, as did a surprise freshman, Seth Woodward. Josh and Seth were cut out of the same mold, guys with lots of integrity that always gave you all they had, exactly what you want to build and maintain a quality program. Seth was amazingly consistent for a freshman. Young runners rarely seem to come up with good races every meet. It takes a certain amount of confidence and experience to mature to that level. Seth, however, was super-fit when practice began and often set the pace during workouts. He opened the season as our second man, running fifth overall at the Marshall County Invitational. Our top runner that day was actually Lanham. Defending state champ Charlie Moore was coming off of a tough series of bangs and bruises that had really hampered his training. Around the fourth of July, Charlie walked out the door of his family's trailer and was hit in the eye with a bottle rocket. After a few weeks he recovered, but Charlie's training was interrupted again by a bruised knee, another accident at home. Finally, Charlie put together several days of solid training prior to the season-opener; however, ten minutes before the meet began we decided to hold him out. There had been a break in a waterline near his home a few days earlier, and Charlie looked a bit green around the gills, apparently a victim to drinking some impure water.

The early season was certainly a challenge for Charlie; however, by our fifth meet, the Franklin County Invitational, he was once again fit. Charlie was beaten by three seconds but still matched his winning time from the '93 state finals, 15:27. Lanham, Brown, Woodward, and Skillman all dipped under 17:00, and a 16:26 three mile average indicated that things were beginning to click for us. Our team depth was also coming along. We dominated the City-County Championship, pushing twelve guys into the top nineteen spots. We would need that depth. Talented junior Derek Brown was injured a few days later and would miss our last three meets.

Folks talk about team chemistry and such. There's something to it. Brown, Woodward, Skillman, and improving junior Brandon Swope had all begun to pack together very well behind frontrunner Moore and Chris Lanham. Taking one guy out of the mix seemed to take a big bite out of their joint confidence. Without Derek, we ran fifth in the Meet of Champions and fell victim to North Hardin in the regional. Still, we felt very optimistic about our chances of bringing home state meet hardware from Lexington a week later.

State Meet '94

Even though Charlie Moore had won the state meet in '93, many folks were reluctant to pin that champion tag on him. Kentucky's golden boy of '94 seemed to be Louisville Male senior Ryan Knight. Indeed, Ryan was a terrific runner and great person. He had beaten Charlie by three seconds at the Franklin County meet on the Horse Park grounds, and this looked to be a super dual.

As expected, the two favorites found one another just meters into the race. The pair hit the mile in 4:50 and was stride for stride when they popped out of the woods a quarter mile later. The crowd got what they wanted as Charlie and Ryan's dual split two miles in a swift 9:58. Just past that point, they hit the hill that served Jeramy Kazlauskas so well in '92. Knight tried to test Charlie's resolve heading up the incline, but it was in vain as he could not open a significant gap. On top of the hill, Charlie returned the favor, and Knight could not respond. Charlie made the race his own from that point and romped home in a swift 15:11, proving he was Kentucky's premier harrier for the second year in a row.

Sophomore Chris Lanham's performance was one of the surprises of the day. Chris was very competitive and one of those guys who was never at a loss for something to say. He ran so smoothly that his form often belied the intensity of his effort. Chris hit splits of 4:59 and 10:24 on the way to an outstanding sixth place finish. His response? "I should have gotten the three guys in front of me." Chris would have had to run 17 seconds faster to do so, but you have to love that mindset! Up and coming Brandon Swope further proved himself with a stout 36th place in 16:52; meanwhile, freshmen Seth Woodward had a day not soon to be forgotten. As he passed my vantage point, late in the race, Seth had worked his way up to about the top 35 and seemed to be in good shape. Just moments later, unknown to me, Seth's body began having a huge fuss with his mind. Coming down the slope toward the finish, he began to stumble and had an exaggerated forward lean, trying to stay balanced. About 200 meters from the finish, Seth fell for the first time. Clearly disoriented, instinct told him, "get to the line." Several times Seth went down, got back to his feet and struggled forward a few steps, only to fall again, jostled by other competitors sprinting by. That last stretch of the race must have felt like a marathon for Seth as he literally crawled on his hands and knees the last 15 meters to the white chalk that represented assistance and relief, a 69th place finish. We are still unsure what happened that day; it was probably a mixture of some virus coming on and maybe some dehydration. After an extended stay in the first aid tent, Seth wobbled back to our team area. Competitors don't always get what they deserve in athletics, but the strength gained in the struggle serves them well down the road some-where, usually over and over, in the experience we call life.

Our basketball convert, Josh Skillman, had a decent performance (52nd-17:08). Josh and Seth had worked very well together the second half of the season. Seth's struggles seemed to affect Josh's race. Still, I would love to have a team full of Josh Skillmans every year.

Our score of 122 was good for fourth place, only 16 points out of second. Certainly, a healthy Derek Brown, along with Seth finishing upright, would have made a huge difference in the complexion of the meet. As a way of putting an exclamation mark on a tough outing, Seth Woodward regurgitated on the bus trip back to Owensboro. Sometimes you just have one of those days!

Charlie wound up his brilliant career by qualifying for Footlocker Nationals. He earned a cross country and track scholarship to my alma mater, Eastern Kentucky University. Charlie graduated four years later with a degree in law enforcement. Cross country literally changed Charlie Moore's life!

Charlie Moore leads Ryan Knight near the two mile
mark on the way to his second state title.

— 1995 —

The first half of the 1995 season brought modest success for the "Raging Red Line." Through the first six meets, we had three wins, a second, and a third, all in invitationals. We were a solid team, but still a ways from being a serious threat for the state title.

In mid-September, Mike West, who had taken over the basketball program, told me that he had a kid running pretty well in pre-season conditioning. He said Derrick Roby had run something like a 5:30 mile and encouraged me to take a look at him. I shrugged it off since we were already well into our season. The next week Mike told me Derrick had run in the 5:20's, and I still resisted contacting him. It did remind me, however, of Charlie Moore coming out late in 1992 and Jon Eriksen in 1993, both making a huge impact. There was no way lightning could strike three times for us! Just a few days later Coach West informed me that Derrick ran 5:12. Finally, I figured maybe I had better listen. I contacted Derrick and his father, and a couple of days later Derrick hesitantly joined the team. Since it was less than six weeks until state meet and we didn't have many meets left, I allowed Derrick to begin competing in races right away. I figured if we could get him hooked on the sport he may really help us as a senior the following year.

About a week after Derrick joined us, I took the varsity team to Birmingham, Alabama for the Vulcan Classic and sent Derrick and our jayvee team to the Marshall County Invitational where our girls' coach and his team was competing. I entered our jayvee guys in the varsity race there, and Derrick actually ran pretty well, finishing the 5,000 meters in 31st place out of 148 runners. He was less than enthusiastic, however, and told his dad on the way home that he thought it might be better to just resume conditioning for basketball season. We were able to convince Derrick to stick it out, and his athleticism and super competitive nature soon began to show in both practice and meets. Derrick quickly worked his way into a varsity spot and was improving with every race.

'95 State Championship . . . The Perfect Race

As the title races approached, Louisville St. Xavier had established itself as the dominant team in Kentucky. As a matter of fact, going into the state meet they were unbeaten and ranked 25th in the nation by *Harrier* magazine. Everyone in the state felt like the championship was a foregone conclusion with St X the prohibitive favorite . . . everyone felt that way . . . except us! Two weeks earlier, at the Meet of Champions (a state preview of sorts) on the state meet course, St X beat us 53 to 83. After viewing video of that meet however, I was convinced we had a shot at them. I knew Derrick had a couple of more weeks to improve and could move up several places, and I felt we had better leg speed as a team than St X. If we could get the confrontation to come to down to the last 400 meters or so, it could be interesting! We came up with a race plan to pack it out smooth and hit the mile around 5:15, be very aggressive to the 4,000 meter mark, cruise the next quarter-mile across the top of the course, prepared for an all guts effort for the last 500 meters that led to the finish line.

There is a big difference in running to win and running not to lose, and we felt all the pressure would be on St. X. Still, they were experienced and confident, and it would take a near-perfect race to beat them. The team we sent to the starting line consisted of senior Brandon Swope, juniors Derrick Roby and Chris Lanham, sophomores Seth Woodward and Robert McCann, and freshmen David Christian and Jason McGuffin.

At the crack of the starter's pistol, Swope, Roby, Lanham, Woodward, and Christian moved as one, while McCann and McGuffin worked together. True to form, the St Xavier team went out packed and strong. About one kilometer into the race their guys had already positioned themselves toward the front with a team score less than 100 points. At the same time, we were well grouped and our places at that point would have given us over 200 points. We entered the tree lined trail at the mile mark with our top five all between 5:16 and 5:20 and were moving through the field well. This part of the course is about 400 meters long. At the end of the trail, runners come out near a creek that lines the bottom of the layout, and a tremendous crowd gets their first real view of how the race is progressing, the air exploding with their cheers. It really picks the runners up and gives them a fresh shot of adrenaline.

At that point in the race, our pack had really closed on St. X, and people were beginning to consider that perhaps the team race might be a bit closer than predicted. The next half mile or so of the course is basically a straightaway beginning with an incline that goes away from the creek and then a parallel straightaway that brings the field back toward the crowd. Our guys took turns leading our group with Swope, then Roby, and then Lanham all at the point of our pack but never far apart. As we came back down the hill and toward the crowd, about 3,000 meters into the race, our top five were all within an unbelievable three seconds of each other. We had infiltrated the St. X pack and now the chase was almost dead even. Spectators were shocked at what they were seeing. Sensing an upset, they really picked us up. Now, we had a *race!*

Daviess County and St. X seemed to run stride for stride for the next mile, and it began to look like a dual meet as both teams' runners pushed farther and farther toward the front of the field. Beginning down the hill that initiated the last 500 meters, the race was too close to call. Our guys had nailed the plan up to this point. In that last straightaway runners from both teams basically held their place. However, about 100 meters from the finish, Derrick Roby gained two critical spots, kicking past St. Xavier's second and third men. Chris Lanham led us across the line in sixth place. Unbelievably, lightning struck for the third time! Roby, who actually knew nothing about cross country six weeks earlier, finished ninth. Freshman David Christian gave the state a glimpse of what was to come as he finished an outstanding 12th. Just behind him in 13th came our senior, Brandon Swope. As Brandon crossed the line, he looked back over his shoulder to find our fifth man. A sense of relief came over Brandon's face when he saw Seth Woodward just a few yards back. Seth's 16th place sealed the deal. Our guys had run the perfect race with a 15.7 second #1-#5 split and had pulled off one of the great upsets in Kentucky State Meet history, a five point victory over an excellent and very classy St. Xavier squad, who had put all five of their scorers in the top nineteen. Our 15.7 second split was the smallest of any state champion team in the nation that year.

Meanwhile . . . back at the ranch . . . my wife Pam was really under the weather and stayed home, the only state meet she has missed since I have been coaching. As soon as I could borrow a phone, I gave her a call and nonchalantly said, "Well, we won." Knowing how dominant St. Xavier had been all season, Pam thought I was kidding. Then I gave her the details. Hearing my excitement and feeling my emotion, Pam starting crying. State championships are good for just about anything that ails you!

Brandon Swope (#15), Derrick Roby, and Chris Lanham (#11) lead a tight Daviess County pack near the 3,000 meter mark of the 1995 state meet.

Derrick Roby gains critical spots as he sprints toward
the finish line in the 1995 state meet.

— 1996 —

Coaching can be like riding a roller coaster with your eyes closed.
Things are going smoothly and then you're hit with a wild hill or a crazy
curve, often in the form of a teen-age decision. Cross country is a tough,
uncomfortable sport that takes tons of commitment over a high school
season and career. Quite frankly, there are easier things to do, and kids
today have so many more options available than when I was growing
up. For that reason, I learned several years ago that it is easier to survive
the unexpected twists if you stay somewhat neutral in your pre-season
expectations, work hard, and wait for events to unfold.

On paper, our '96 team could arguably have been as good as any in Daviess
County history. With four returnees who finished in the top sixteen at state,

and some good fresh talent coming in, we seemed headed toward back-to-back championships. We were disappointed, however, when two of our top four decided not to run. Many times coaches lament those losses and spend so much energy on the "what ifs" that they cheat the athletes they have.

I always loved the scene from the movie *Hoosiers* where Gene Hackman was addressing the school's student body while introducing his team for the season. There was much concern because local legend Jimmy Chitwood was not playing. The chant "we want Jimmy" began to echo through the gym. Hackman silenced the crowd and brought them back into focus with a statement to the effect of, "we cannot be concerned with who we are not, but rather who we are!" That's what we had to do in '96.

There was plenty of reason for excitement surrounding our program. David Christian was coming off of a terrific freshman year and looked as if he might be ready to challenge for a few individual wins. Derrick Roby was now a totally committed runner in the fall and spring as well as a starter on our basketball team during the winter. I expected Jason McGuffin and Robert McCann to make significant gains, and we felt a few younger guys would step up.

Tennessee Classic–David's Coming Out and Mark's Coming In Party

I had never used a middle school student on our high school varsity, but this year I made an exception. My oldest son, Mark, an eighth-grader, had developed very early as a distance runner and had a pure passion for the sport. Our middle school coach, Artie Marx, and I agreed that Mark would train with my team but run three or four middle school races before being pulled up to compete with us. After winning each of those meets by a minute or more, I decided to throw Mark into the high school waters at the Tennessee Classic.

Our guys have always loved the Tennessee meet. It was a flat, fast three miler, and the kids' times are a reward for their hard work. Going into this meet, the team had won the Daviess County and Apollo Invitationals and finished fourth at Warren East. David Christian had two second place finishes and a win to his credit. The finest runner in all of Kentucky in the early season was Bowling Green junior Matt Tabor, an irrepressible young man with a bubbly personality and a ferocious ability to attack a race. At Warren East, Tabor easily handled the field with a 41 second victory, Christian finishing second.

I wish I knew what gets into a young man's mind when he decides he is going to become a champion! For some it is a gradual process. For others it is a deliberate, almost overnight decision. David Christian decided he wanted to run with Matt Tabor at the Tennessee Classic. Knowing David wasn't going to break Matt's pace out on the course, our goal was to get the deal to come down to a sprint.

The race was sensational. From the get-go, David and Matt hooked up and began pounding the pace. Stride for stride at the mile (4:49) and two mile (10:01) marks, David's race plan was playing out perfectly. Neither runner would concede even an inch. When the pair hit a slight downhill 400 meters from the finish, it was like two slugging heavyweights entering the 15th round. On cue, David threw his final punch. His piston-like efficiency broke Matt's longer, powerful stride, and David willed his way to a four second victory, setting a new course record (15:11) in the process.

It was a defining moment in David's career. From that day on, he knew what it would take to be one of the South's finest runners. David decided the thrill of victory was worth the pain he had to run through to get there. A tiger was born!

David's "coming out" day was Mark Rowe's "coming in" day. Mark took advantage of his first significant varsity competition by finishing 21st (16:32) out of 260 competitors . . . certainly not your average middle school performance. Our team finished a strong third place and left that meet with a growing confidence that we could once again contend for the Kentucky state title.

Late Season

Louisville Trinity was ranked first in Kentucky and having an excellent season. Rich Rostel's teams were always superbly conditioned, well-grouped, and ran very intelligently . . . a great reflection of a terrific coach. We were getting better with each race, and the Meet of Champions in late October suggested the state meet could be close. David won the race on a cool, rainy day in 16:11. Mark astonished everyone with an outstanding race (8th-16:59). Right behind him was Derrick Roby, in the same time. Trinity got the measure of us 54–70, but we were competing well as the championship season rolled around.

Although we sent two seniors, Derrick Roby and Chris Matheny, and junior Robert McCann to the starting line in the regional at Hopkinsville, the balance of our lineup was a virtual youth movement. We were counting on big races from sophomores David Christian and Jason McGuffin, freshman Chad Kimberlin, and Mark Rowe, our middle schooler. They delivered! Christian set a new course record, touring the 5,000 meters in 15:48, and along with Roby (4th-16:30), McGuffin (5th-16:37), Rowe (6th-16:43), and Kimberlin (10th-17:12) produced an unbeatable 26 point effort and a very stout 16:34 average for our five scorers. Late-season confidence is an invaluable weapon, and we headed toward Lexington on a high note.

State Meet '96.

We always do some mental preparation the last couple of weeks of the season. We want our athletes to consider their race but not to dwell on it constantly. At our home during state meet week, Mark was like a cat on a hot tin roof. He could hardly contain his excitement, looking forward to his first high school championship race. Mark must've watched the commentary on legendary running icon Steve Prefontaine about fifteen times as he dreamed of conquest in the Bluegrass. Admittedly, I was a bit concerned about this, but decided to say nothing and see how the situation played out.

The week turned very wet and cold. Three straight days of rain prior to the race had the state course resembling a flagged-off hog lot. There were huge puddles of water and mud everywhere; conditions certainly seemed to favor the older, stronger runners. None of that seemed to matter to David Christian. He threw every bit of his 5'6" and 110 pounds, mostly heart I am sure, into the challenge. David dreamed of following in the footsteps of two of his Daviess County heroes, Jeramy Kazlauskas and Charlie Moore. Putting 100 yards between himself and Trinity's Scott Holzknecht in the last half of the race, David streaked to his tenth straight win of the season and more importantly, the individual state title. Dependable Derrick Roby finished eighth, and Jason McGuffin came through with an excellent race in 14th place.

Mark's race was a struggle. He was hoping for a finish in the top 10; however, the mud and slippery turf seemed to be more than his body was ready for. Later, we talked about his possible loss of mental energy during the week from watching the Pre video. It was like he had already run the race fifteen times before the gun ever went off. Still, 25th place as an eighth-grader was an outstanding accomplishment. Chad Kimberlin finished our scoring in 45th overall. Versatile Chris Matheny ran three seconds behind him. Chris would become a double state champion the next spring in track, winning the 110 meter high hurdles and the long jump.

Although it was Trinity's day as far as the team race went, I could not have been more proud of our men. They had overcome the loss of teammates, the pressure of being defending champs, and relative inexperience to finish as the state runner-up.

David Christian wins his first of three individual state championships.

— 1997 —

If you are going to build a team, it is nice to start with the defending state champion. David Christian followed his super sophomore fall campaign with an excellent track season, winning state crowns in the 1600 and 3200 meter runs and as a member of our victorious 3200 meter relay foursome. Another man on that relay team was Jason McGuffin. Jason's real surprise in track, however, was kicking into an unexpected runner-up spot (to David) in the 1600 meters in Lexington (4:22.9). Mark Rowe also was coming off of an excellent spring, having posted a 9:58 for 3200 meters as an eighth-grader.

We certainly felt our top three were capable of high finishes in the big show come November. The trio could be compared to McKay Mattingly, Scott Eckstein, and Mike Rhodes in '78, perhaps the premier front-running threesome I had ever coached. Of course, it takes five to score in this sport. Our support group was somewhat of a project, but very capable. Through the fall, eight different men would fill the #4-#7 positions, including seniors Robert McCann and Pat Riley, junior Blake Main, sophomores Daniel Riherd, Austin Swope, Chris Shown, and Chad Kimberlin, and freshman Jeff Goodman.

The Daviess County Classic proved to be quite a season opening test, specifically in the form of some excellent individuals and the very hot and sunny late August day. As expected, Christian, Rowe, and McGuffin were among the frontrunners when scores were tallied; however, David's 10 meet winning streak from '96 was broken. Matt Tabor of Bowling Green was razor-sharp, totally ignoring the weather and gapping his nearest pursuer by 31 seconds while collecting a course record 16:07. Matt's teammate, Justin Griffin, and Union County's Aaron Tucker also sneaked in ahead of David. Still, I had no doubt that David would piece together another strong string of victories at some point in the meets to come. Kimberlin (13th) and Main (25th) combined with our 4–6–7 top three to provide a satisfying win.

After fairly easy triumphs the following two weekends, we found ourselves once again at the super-competitive Tennessee Classic in Music City, USA, the site of Christian's break-out race in '96. Again, Christian (3rd-15:26), McGuffin (10th-15:51), and Rowe (12th-15:54) gave Daviess County the lowest score through three men of any team in the forty-six school meet. Nationally ranked Memphis Houston's five proved to be the class of the field with 83 points. Oak Ridge, Tennessee (142) edged us for second, going to the sixth man tiebreaker. David ran 36 seconds closer to Matt Tabor than in our season opener. Both, however, were schooled by Brett Baddorf, the stocky, tough–minded senior leader of the Houston squad, victorious in 15:11. Ironically, Brett would eventually become a teammate of my son, Mark, at Samford University in Birmingham.

Birmingham is exactly where we found ourselves during the first weekend of October, competing in the tremendously talented field of the Vulcan Classic. Four teams ranked in the top dozen nationally were on hand. Those schools were certainly the class of the field with Nevada Union, California taking the overall honors, followed by Memphis Houston, Xavier of Connecticut and Brookwood, Georgia. As good as those teams were we still put our third finisher (Jason McGuffin) in front of Houston and Brookwood's third. Again, Brett Baddorf dominated individually running 15:23 over the tough three mile path. Christian picked himself up from a fall about 150 meters into the race for a third place finish. This was to be David's last loss of the season as he was about to set some trails ablaze with some sizzling performances.

David's siege on the record book began with the City-County Championships. Ignoring sore calves from the hilly Vulcan race, David bettered his own record on the equally challenging layout at Ben Hawes Park. He then missed Charlie Moore's course standard of 16:09 by four seconds at the Marshall County Invitational. He would get another shot three weeks later in the regional.

The Meet of Champions on October 25th was critical for many reasons. First, it was at the State site. Furthermore, most of Kentucky's best programs would compete there. As it turned out, nine of the top 10 teams and twenty of the first 25 individual state meet finishers also participated in this competition. We often used the Meet of Champions results to develop our strategy for the championship.

On this day, the race belonged to talented and tightly packed Louisville Trinity. Showing why they were considered Kentucky's finest crew, the Shamrocks accumulated just 57 points. The logjam that followed had everyone looking for a tough team competition when all the marbles would be on the line two weeks later. Covington Scott finished with 93 points, and on their heels were Daviess County (110), Greenwood (111) and Covington Catholic (112). In the dash for individual honors, it was all David Christian. There seemed to be something about the Kentucky Horse Park that always put a bit more giddy-up in David's gallop. Cranking out rather hasty mile (4:48) and two mile (9:52) splits, David gobbled up Thomas Murley's course record, running 15:40 on the layout which had been extended from 3 miles to 5,000 meters. Jason McGuffin came through with perhaps his finest hour of the year, flying into the chute in third place (16:20). Mark Rowe's 16:36 and tenth position in the 259 man field further confirmed the toughness and talent of our lead group.

Regional and State

People often judge a program by how they perform when the pressure is greatest. A team can run well all season, but unless they repeat that effort during the championship races, the success seems shallow. I have always felt the best way to prepare for the state meet is to demand a great regional effort. I have seen coaches with dominant teams back off in their state qualifier, supposedly saving their athletes' legs, psyche or whatever, for state. I don't agree with that philosophy. It makes no sense to me for a team to work for months, to be sharpest over the last two weeks . . . and then deemphasize one of those competitions.

The Panthers were certainly on the prowl the first day of November on the Marshall County campus. David Christian got the course record he had missed three weeks earlier, touring the 5,000 meters in 16:06. Jason McGuffin and Mark Rowe made it a 1–2–3 sweep with Chad Kimberlin 8th, Blake Main 10th, Dan Riherd 15th, and Robert McCann 20th; an excellent 24 point team effort.

A week later, in Lexington, the air was cold and the ground wet; seemingly unfavorable conditions for fast times. Christian, needless to say, wanted to make it two in a row, but it would be tough for him to realize his second goal of another course record. Nevertheless, David pressed through his first mile in 4:51 and was 9:55 at two miles, three seconds behind his record pace from the Meet of Champions. With a commanding lead in the late stages, David's competition became the clock. Moments later, David emphatically punched his fist into the air as he crossed under that clock with two seconds to spare . . . 15:38!

Jason McGuffin and Mark Rowe found their way to the awards chairs (top fifteen) with inspiring runs of 16:23 (6th) and 16:34 (12th), respectively. Louisville Trinity successfully defended their championship trophy while Covington Catholic edged us out of runner-up honors by just five points.

— 1998 —

Additions

We had plenty of reasons to be excited looking toward the '98 campaign. Our top six men returned from the fine '97 crew. A couple of additions would create quite a challenge for varsity spots.

A few months earlier, David Christian and Mark Rowe noticed a classmate regularly scooting at a brisk pace around the perimeter of Hillcrest Golf Course. Chris Cox had a baseball background, but decided to forego the sport his junior and senior year. Chris was about 5'10, maybe 130 pounds of lean muscle and natural ability. Running came easy to him. It didn't take much for the guys, and especially David, to convince Chris to join us. After all, as Chris put it, "To have a state champ call you up and ask you to come out for the team is very flattering. I thought 'maybe he thinks I'm OK.'" A few jaunts over some training routes were all it took for us realize that Chris was going to be more than just "OK." Your runners are often your best recruiters; in Chris, they had picked a plum!

In the middle of the summer I received a phone call from Randy Swann, who lived about 50 miles to our south. Randy's family was moving to Owensboro and his son, Devin, would be enrolling at Daviess County. This was *news!* Devin, you see, was the defending Class AA (medium-size schools) state champion for Muhlenberg North. Devin joining our squad was like bringing Citation into the barn with Secretariat and his thoroughbred buddies. (It's a horse thing!)

Exciting as the possibilities were, I also knew we could expect repercussions, figuring there would be accusations of recruiting and cheating going around. Those allegations began almost immediately. It was almost funny how many supposed experts concerning our program surfaced on websites and such. I even got a call from the Kentucky High School

Athletic Association commissioner. We chose to deal with all the rumors by training hard and going about our own business.

So . . . do we recruit? Yessireebob! Do we cheat? No way! Let me share my design for getting athletes out for cross country and track. Before each season, I pray that the Lord will send the guys He wants me to work with. Then . . . I hit my recruiting grounds . . . the hallways of Daviess County High School. When the team is in place, I have a great responsibility to the athletes God has put in my path. Not only do I expect their best, but they have the right to expect mine.

Up the Ante

David Christian's dad, Mike, did an extraordinary job of everything from encouraging and motivating David to dealing with the numerous recruiters that wanted his son's talents to find a home on their particular campus the next few seasons. Mike became quite knowledgeable on the ins and outs of our sport, and we dubbed him the team "information man."

For a team to be superior during final exams, it needs some thorough tests along the way. The best high school harrier in the United States in '98 was Wheeling, Illinois' Jorge Torres. His twin brother, Eduardo, was nearly Jorge's equal, and their team was ranked in the top fifteen nationally. We decided that running against them would definitely be a great measuring stick, both for our team and our top individuals. I put our information man on the assignment and Mike came up with Wheeling's schedule. We had an opening the same weekend that Wheeling was competing in the Lake Park Invitational near Chicago and incorporated the meet into our plans for the fall.

Opening with a Bang

Anticipation built during a high-quality preseason of training, and our opener, the Daviess County Classic, seemed to set the tone for the season. Christian blasted the course record on a 90 degree day, running 16:04. Swann was second with a quick 16:39, just holding off Rowe (16:47). Chris Cox threw down a 17:26 in his first meet ever, finishing eighth. When Blake Main sprinted home in 14th, we had scored a very low 28 points, making a statement to teams across Kentucky that this was going to be a special year for the Raging Red Line.

At the Warren East Invitational a week later, the weather was even hotter, pushing 100 degrees.

Our men were equally dominant as the same five scorers romped in 1–2–4–6–11 for 24 points and a 16:20 average. Although I don't allow gloating and bragging, we were feeling pretty doggone good about ourselves and walked away from the course with chests stuck out like proud peacocks. The team would put up even more imposing numbers in late-season get-togethers, but first we had a lesson to learn.

"Wherefore let him that thinketh he standeth take heed lest he fall"
1 Corinthians 10:12

A Visit to York

After dominating performances in our first two competitions, we were anxious to head up North toward Chicago for the Lake Park Invitational.

I have always respected the wonderful contributions that Joe Newton of Elmhurst (Illinois) York High School has given to our sport. Joe has become one of those larger than life figures in American distance running. I would dare say more coaches in our country have learned about distance running from reading Newton's philosophy and techniques than anyone.

Most experts would agree that York has been the premier schoolboy cross country program in the United States over the past four decades. While they were not scheduled to compete in the Lake Park meet, knowing we would be within a few miles of their school on our trip was too much of an opportunity to pass. Most of our guys knew about York's tradition and were excited about possibly walking through the school, perhaps catching a glimpse of the legend himself. Unannounced, we pulled into York's campus just before the end of school on Friday. I suppose we were a bit naive coming from Kentucky, but the security at their school was quite impressive. Still, after a visit to the office and a mild interrogation, we were allowed a mini-tour and finally escorted to an area just outside the gym where Coach Newton was conducting his "first shift" practice. Our guys were pretty much in awe. For some of them, it was like an Elvis sighting! I introduced our entourage to Coach Newton and considering we crashed his party, he was very hospitable. Coach began to tell us about his team-and singled out his leaders, which included a promising sophomore whose name running aficionados will recognize - Donald Sage. Our guys were all ears. Seeing he had a captive audience, Joe went into the entertainment mode, enlightening us, among other things, about his kinfolks buried in Kentucky.

In the middle of his spiel, Coach Newton told one of his managers, "Go get my friend from Kentucky a shirt." A minute or so later the boy came back with an order form, which brought the gruff but somehow good-natured ire of his coach. "I didn't say a . . . form . . . I said a shirt!" Moments later the manager came back with a long-sleeved York cross country shirt. Coach smiled as he presented it to me as a souvenir of our visit.

Through it all, his guys sat quietly and respectfully, waiting for their orders. Many people criticize Coach Newton for his high mileage techniques and the tough demands he throws on his athletes. From my viewpoint, although we were there just briefly, the York athletes were disciplined, organized, and held their coach in very high esteem. The shadow Joe Newton casts has raised the bar, and we found out the next day that cross country in the greater Chicago area is super competitive.

Lake Park Invitational

Jorge and Ed Torres were the real deal. Both were very pleasant young men who, like most cross country runners, aren't going to overwhelm you with their physical stature. When they ran, however, the image projected was amazing. They looked bigger, stronger, and downright intimidating with the dogged fervor of their effort. Run they did that day! Jorge won the three mile race in a very fleet 14:36, besting his brother by nine seconds. Christian (4th-15:20) and Swann (5th-15:25) led our charge, but we were somewhat flat overall and came in a distant fifth place team-wise with 123 points; Wheeling set the standard with 47.

The proud peacocks of a week earlier walked away from the course more like whipped puppies. I was somewhat disappointed with our performance, but the guys seemed even more so . . . as well as a bit embarrassed. On the long trip back to Kentucky, it seemed a joint resolve set in. After that, our team was different; the workouts were extremely focused, the intensity wretched up, and the goals extremely lofty.

Part of the '98 gang included: (l. to r.) Jordan Tong, Devin Swann, Chris Cox, David Christian, Mark Rowe, Blake Main, and Jason McGuffin.

Back in the Saddle

Our men couldn't wait to "lace 'em up" a week later, as the always stiff challenge of the Tennessee Classic awaited. Temperatures climbed into the 90's as runners from fifty-four schools sized up one another on the starting line. Typically, a team score somewhere in the neighborhood of 100 points would win this huge meet . . . this wasn't a typical day! Four minutes and forty five seconds into the race, David Christian, Devin Swann, and Mark Rowe crossed the mile mark running 1–2–3 with Chris Cox, Jason McGuffin, and Blake Main close behind. Two miles later, a seemingly unending stream of athletes poured across the final meters of the turf and into the finish chute. The Raging Red Line was amazing. I barely needed all my toes and fingers to add up our team score. OK . . . I'm exaggerating a bit . . . but the Panthers did put on quite a cross country clinic. Christian (1st), Swann (2nd), Rowe (5th), Cox (12th), and McGuffin (25th) averaged 15:57 (3 miles) for an eye-popping score of 45 points.

Call it, if you will, the "lake effect," carried over from the trip to Chicago. What a difference a week made!

Reaching New Heights

The effect carried on as we rolled into October posting a perfect score in the four team City-County Meet. What happened next was extraordinary. Marshall County set up scoring in their invitational a bit differently. There was just a varsity race, and each squad could enter unlimited numbers. They took each school's top five finishers and scored them as the "A" team; the next five, the "B" team; numbers 11–15 the "C" team and so on. There were twenty-two "A" teams entered and 241 total competitors. The Panthers were excellent. Our #6-#10 men, consisting of Blake Main, Daniel Riherd, Wes Aull, Chris Shown, and Derek Wells combined for 115 points and finished second . . . overall! The only five that bested them was our "A" team. Coming into the meet, David Christian held the course record of 16:06. He and Devin Swann both went out after it, hitting one mile in 4:50. David pulled away the second mile splitting 9:52 and obliterated the record with a blistering 15:43. Devin barely missed the old standard, running 16:11. Sophomore Mark Rowe came on very strong in the final mile, posting a third place 16:22. With Chris Cox fifth (16:44) and Jason McGuffin sixth (16:49), the Raging Red Line scored an outrageous 17 points, the lowest any of my teams have ever scored in a major invitational. To put that into perspective, remember that 15 points (1–2–3–4–5) is a perfect score in cross country and 27 points cannot lose a dual (two team) meet.

Finally . . . They Meet

There is always lots of buzz in the cross country circles across Kentucky. As the season progressed, that talk centered more and more on the highly anticipated match-up of two-time defending state champion Louisville Trinity and Daviess County.

Although we were in the midst of a most memorable season, the Shamrocks were rolling along themselves. Like us, they were unbeaten among in-state competition and very mature and experienced, running on the strength of six seniors and a junior. On the first weekend of October, they had made a "laugher" of the Vulcan Classic in Birmingham, winning by almost 100 points.

The showdown finally came about at the Meet of Champions, the last regular season contest on a beautiful day at the Kentucky Horse Park. Although we respected Trinity and their accomplishments over the two previous seasons, our men pounced on the first mile with a seeming reckless abandon; Christian, Swann, Cox, and Rowe all splitting 5:00 or better. By two miles the issue had been decided, and at 5,000 meters Christian was grand marshal of the parade, establishing a new course record of 15:19. With Swann (2nd-15:44), Cox (4th-16:06), Rowe (9th-16:19), and McGuffin (18th-16:42) our red and white pack overwhelmed the nearly 300 runner field with 34 points. Our 16:02 average remains the lowest any squad has ever produced on the state meet course.

Crank It Up!

With the maturity and talent we had, workouts were often special to behold. We do a series of concentrated sessions the last month of the season which involve very fast runs on the roads close to school. The courses are meticulously measured for accuracy, and records are kept for comparison to past teams. We lace up our racing shoes and watch the training sparks fly; the intensity rivaling that of our best races.

This year, in particular, individual and team confidence soared as our guys hit numerous personal bests. Mile and two mile times on these days included: Christian (4:20, 8:57), Swann (4:26, 9:19), McGuffin (4:39, 9:33), Cox (4:30, 9:35) and Rowe (4:37, 9:38). We were ready!

Regional

The dazzling Meet of Champions effort would be hard to match, but regional always gets the juices flowing. It seemed fitting that this team and David Christian, in particular, would get the opportunity to run one more meet in front of our home crowd. Those folks were treated to quite a show. On a fall day perfect for running, the Panthers produced perhaps the most dominant performance in regional history.

As the human train rounded the last corner and chugged into the chute, seven of the first eight "cars" were painted in red and white. David could have run comfortably, saving his legs for state and still would not have hurt the team. Instead, he chose to bust a move just beyond the mile mark, embrace the pain, and stamp an indelible mark on the meet. David absolutely destroyed the course record, covering the harsh 5,000 meters in a stunning 15:46 . . . a record that could stand for a good while!

'98 State Championship

One final battle loomed in what had been a near perfect season. Although *Harrier* magazine labeled Daviess County the 17th best team in the United States, the big Kentucky-shaped trophy was what mattered most. The ranking, the dual-meet-like invitational scores, the overwhelming favorite tag . . . all added to the pressure squarely on the shoulders of our young men. Louisville Trinity was not going to relinquish their champion label without a fight, and they had plenty of motivation.

Earlier in the season Trinity's long-time coach, Rich Rostel, passed away. Rich was the most successful cross country coach in Kentucky history. I had the privilege of spending significant time with Rich as roommates at a track clinic a couple of years earlier. We shared training ideas, talked about our families, discussed each of our individual relationships with the Lord, and developed a friendship that had previously been just a distant respect, forged from years of rivalry between our programs. Rich was truly one of the good guys in our sport, and his teams were a class act. I phoned Rich and talked with him less than a week before he lost a tough battle with cancer. Let there be no doubt, Rich Rostel won the race of life, and I am sure that he is enjoying his reward.

With somewhat mixed emotions I sent our team to their starting box. In a sense, it seemed our guys, as well as Trinity's, could honor Coach Rostel best by giving a supreme effort. The Shamrocks were game and came after us with everything they had, placing six runners in the top 29. Our own sixth man finished 30th. The difference was up front.

David Christian was a blur with splits of 4:41 and 9:41. When he streaked across the finish stripe in an extraordinary 15:10, another course record had fallen. Devin Swann demonstrated his toughness, finishing runner-up in 15:45. As Devin and David cleared the roped-off chute, they were anxious to double back and find their teammates. Mark Rowe (11th), Wes Aull (28th) and Blake Main (30th) had all put together commendable efforts. Jason McGuffin, who had been sixth in the state meet as a junior, fought off the pain of a small broken bone in one foot, finishing 45th. But where was Chris Cox? When I reached the team, they were literally in tears. Their concern baffled me because I had accounted for all seven of our men a couple hundred meters from the finish. After several anxious moments, we found Chris being attended to by the medical staff. He felt heavy legged and arm weary throughout most of the race. In the stretch run dizziness set in, and as Chris crossed the line he collapsed. He was quickly removed from the finish area and taken to first aid. When our guys could not locate Chris in the procession of finishers, they assumed he had dropped out and thought Trinity had possibly beaten us. Chris recuperated and his 15th place effort was more than enough to ensure victory.

Receiving the trophy a short time later, our squad took turns "leaving their mark." This was a tradition that began a couple of years earlier. Our guys bite each regional winning and state champion or runner-up trophy. It sounds goofy, and folks probably wonder why there is so much scarred hardware in the case of our school lobby. That first place wood just has a sweet, sweet flavor!

An Era

While we emphasize the team, we certainly celebrate the individual accomplishments of our runners. David Christian's impact on Kentucky high school running transformed his years into an era to be remembered. After finishing 12th in the state cross country meet as a freshman, David won three straight individual titles. David helped our team win four consecutive regional and two State championships, as well as a state runner-up and third place. He qualified for the Footlocker Nationals as a sophomore and again as a senior. In the 35 meets he represented Daviess County during his final three years of high school, David won 28 times with an incredible average finish of 1.37 and sixteen course records. Add to his cross country exploits three state titles in both the 1600 and 3200 meter runs on the track. David was also a member of our winning 4 x 800 relay teams in Lexington three years in a row. Our track teams won two Kentucky championships and had a runner-up during that time.

Perhaps David's greatest quality was that of making those around him feel important. Time and again I observed David humbly play down his own accomplishments and build others up. True champions are a rare breed and sometimes hard to find. David Christian was a champion!

— The Footlocker Experience —

Kinney-Footlocker Qualifiers

In 1980, the idea of a national high school cross country championship race came to fruition. With Kinney Shoes serving as the primary sponsor, the United States was divided into four regions. Any athlete who runs high school cross country is eligible to participate in his or her respective regional with the top eight finishers in each advancing to the national championship in San Diego. The thirty-two boys and girls (that number has now been expanded to forty each) that make it to the nationals have all their expenses paid and are treated like kings and queens in a four day experience they will never forget. The race is televised on ESPN. The meet is now recognized as the Footlocker Championships after that company took over the main sponsorship in the early '90's, and the whole event has given a terrific boost to high school cross country in the United States.

Kentucky is in the South Region. Our meet is contested over Thanksgiving weekend each year at McAlpine-Greenway Park in Charlotte, North Carolina. The course at McAlpine is basically flat, except for one very significant hill about half way through the layout. The distance is advertised as 3.1 miles (5,000 meters), but I have always felt it may be about 80 or 90 meters short. Times are traditionally faster in Charlotte than any of the other regions. In many ways, the Footlocker region races are tougher than the national finals with the pressure of qualifying and the tremendous numbers in the race. The McAlpine course is a straight shot for about one kilometer before tapering down to a trail that can only handle about four people wide. If a runner is not in about the top

20 by the time he hits the trail, his chances of qualifying for nationals are greatly reduced because of the narrowing of the course and the tremendous pack up front. Typically, the front guys will hit the mile mark in about 4:38 to 4:42 and be around 9:45 or better at two miles. The last 500 meters goes along three sides of a small lake with about a 250 meter straightaway finish that has allowed some ferocious kicks. The event is just a tremendous experience.

Our First Finalist

In '92 we took a group of our runners down to Charlotte, including Jeramy Kazlauskas, who earlier in November captured the Kentucky state title. We felt like Kaz would run well, but it is almost impossible to predict how high a runner may place when athletes from twelve or thirteen states are involved. As the race began, Kaz went out with the front pack and simply stayed there. I had never seen him so focused and intense. Fifteen minutes and twenty nine seconds after the gun went off, Kaz became Daviess County's first national finalist. While there is not much that can compare to winning a team state championship, having one of your athletes finish in the top eight in a Footlocker Regional comes pretty doggone close. You have to see the event to fully appreciate the pure guts effort necessary to advance. As Kaz crossed the finish line in fifth place that day, my eyes swelled with tears and I couldn't speak. I just wanted to grab Jeramy and hug him. I caught his eyes as he was walking through the chute, and I could visibly see the strain of the effort on Kaz' face. After several seconds, he recovered enough to realize what he had done, and he too was overcome with emotion. That's the way these regional races are and why they are among the great events in all of high school sports in this country.

Charlie Meets the Challenge

Two years later, Charlie Moore toed the starting line at the same course. Charlie did not get out as well as Kaz had when he qualified and was stuck in about 20th place as the runners hit the narrow trail a kilometer into the race. He needed to be much closer to the front before the critical hill at the half-way point. The hill tends to separate the runners, and it is very difficult to make up even 30 or 40 yards in the last part of the course with such quality competition. At about the 2,000 meter mark there is a hairpin turn in the course. Somehow, in just a few yards, Charlie moved from his position to the top seven as the pack fought its way through the turn. I couldn't believe it! Charlie never looked back after that and finished the race in a swift time of 15:16 (5th place), just ahead of Texas' Brent Hauser, who went on to be one of the stars of the great Stanford University program.   At the Footlocker meets, reputation and recognition that the elite runners have earned command much respect. Charlie remembers the last 200 meters of the race thinking, "I've seen you (Brent Hauser) on the cover of a magazine–now I'm kicking with you." Moments like that are very special as athletes reflect on their careers.   On this day, Charlie, who had hardly even been out of our county (except for cross country and track meets), gained a bit of reputation himself and earned a trip to San Diego.

David's Determination

David Christian shocked the cross country buffs in the state of Kentucky in' 96 when, as a sophomore, he came home from Lexington as the individual state champion. Although he was very young, we wanted to see how David stacked up with the rest of the South's best runners. David did not yet have great speed, but he possessed a dogged determination and an unwavering confidence in himself. He was another one of those young men that had a knack for shrugging off the pain while running through the many barriers that present themselves over the course of a tough competition. In Charlotte, David stayed within striking distance of the lead pack, flying through the mile and two miles with splits of 4:42 and 9:48 and with 500 yards to go had worked up to the seventh spot overall. We were going nuts! However, two runners passed him and another pulled up even. David fought back in the last 300 yards, regaining the seventh spot. Unleashing an ever-improving kick that would serve him so well in the years ahead, David sprinted across the line in 15:18. We had our third different Footlocker finalist over a span of five years.

Untimely Illness

The following year, '97, David defended his state championship and was in great shape for a return to the Footlocker finals. However, early in the week of the region race, a bad virus kept David in bed for the better part of two days. He simply could not recover quick enough to be a factor that Saturday. David, in true champion form, understood the unfortunate timing of his illness and set his sights on "next year." On the up side, my oldest son, Mark, ran 16:22, winning the freshman race in Charlotte that day in a record time. He became the third Kentucky harrier to hold the freshman record in five years with Thomas Murley from Elizabethtown (a two time Footlocker finalist who later starred at Stanford) and Matthew Tabor from Bowling Green. We were obviously thrilled.

Redemption and Rejection

In '98, after capturing his third straight championship in Kentucky, David Christian took every precaution to stay well and train well. In one particular road workout late that fall, David ran an accurate two miler in 9:05, rested fifteen minutes and ran a mile in 4:26, rested three minutes, and ran another mile in 4:24. We knew David was ready for whatever it would take to be a national qualifier again. Our second runner on the Daviess County team that year was senior Devin Swann, an awesome runner in his own right. Devin actually finished the high school season as runner-up to David in the State Meet. In the same workout as mentioned above, Devin's times were 9:21, 4:33 and 4:43.

Thanksgiving weekend arrived and we were once again in Charlotte. The trip itself was always just a great time because several families of my runners would travel together, eat together, and the ladies, of course, would shop together. It was just a special, special trip each year. On race day '98, we were primed and ready to go. David stayed on the leaders' heels the entire race, finishing third with a time of 15:16 and earning his second nationals trip.

An equally determined Devin Swann was not far behind the leaders throughout the race. With about 600 meters to go, he was in 14th place, and we were thrilled with his effort. Devin, however, was not satisfied. He began running down some of the South's best runners, including a young sophomore from Virginia named Alan Webb (now America's best miler), with a vicious kick and flew across the line in 15:31. Devin thought he had captured the eighth and final qualifying spot. However, he miscounted and actually finished in the one place no runner wanted to be in at Footlocker Regions . . . ninth! Devin was predictably very upset to be so close and not qualify. His effort over the last 600 meters of that North Carolina turf still remains one of the most inspiring finishes I have ever witnessed in all my years of involvement in this great sport. Even in his disappointment, Devin left the race knowing he could compete with some of America's best runners. He and David went on to have very successful college careers as teammates at North Carolina State University

Nationals

Each of our runners who qualified through the years seemed to struggle at the Kinney/Footlocker Nationals, all finishing around 30th place. David Christian improved to 22nd place his second time around as a senior, but still expected a better result. Experience is definitely an ally on the national stage. Those rare runners who qualify two or three times know what to expect from the course, the race, and the four days of activities and excitement that surround the big event. It is interesting that the South Region teams very often seem to run sub par races at the national meet. I have always wondered why.

A few years after his Footlocker experiences, David Christian came up with this premise. "The other three Footlocker regional races are run on somewhat difficult, hilly courses. Those courses are strength oriented layouts. To qualify from the South Region, you must go through McAlpine Park, which is basically flat. What you find is that guys with lots of speed tend to qualify down there. Then they go to San Diego and race on a hilly, strength type course."

Indeed, David's hindsight may be right on target. We really built speed into our guys training for the South Region competitions. I have always felt if the nationals were contested four or five weeks in a row over varying courses, the results would change dramatically each race. I do know that when a young person becomes a Footlocker finalist, they wear a badge of honor and respect that follows them throughout the years. Like so many other young athletes across America, all of our guys were better runners and better people because of the Footlocker experience.

— 1999 —

In '99 we had perhaps the most daunting task any of my teams ever faced. How do you replace the individual state champion, the runner-up, a third runner who finished 6th in Lexington as a junior, another who was 15th, and still another 30th? Yet, that was our chore when the seniors of '98 graduated.

We did have junior Mark Rowe and senior Wes Aull returning, but after that there was no one with significant varsity experience. Imagine my excitement when we kicked off the season (the Daviess County Classic) with Mark winning the individual title and five more Panthers stuffed into the top 12 positions. Our 28 points actually matched the '98 squad's total in the same meet.

Victories the next two weekends, at the Warren East and Apollo invitationals, further validated that we had reloaded and could be a serious threat. The Apollo meet was an especially exciting day for our family. Not only did Mark continue his pacesetting trend, but younger brother Matt also jumped up and captured the middle school race over a talented field.

Daviess County parent Bill Swope encourages eventual winner Mark Rowe as he heads up "Goliath" in the 1999 DC Classic.

Friends and Rivals

The young season had already taken on an interesting twist. My old buddy, Jeff Miller, had taken the head coaching position at Apollo. Jeff and I logged countless miles together through the years. We were teammates at Owensboro High School, ran road races and marathons together, and . . . in a phase of questionable sanity during the summer of '75 . . . Jeff and I, along with Craig Hopkins, even trotted through a 50 miler, just to say we had done it. Jeff was an outstanding harrier in both high school and later in college at Louisiana State University. Jeff was my assistant track coach at Daviess County for a few years, and I just could not get comfortable seeing him in Apollo blue. The local media really began to play up the rivalry between our two teams, and Jeff did, indeed, have the Eagles running as well as any Apollo team in several years.

A Tough Opponent

Although we had flown out of the gate, we were beginning to lose some battles off the course. The summer of '99 was desperately dry, and the drought continued into the fall. The ground was rock hard and cracked, and the grass withered, making training on turf as unforgiving as on the road. Several of our athletes developed stress points in their legs, and at times our training entourage resembled the Tour de France.

Nevertheless, several guys in their first year of varsity experience were really beginning to come up with nice performances. Junior Jordan Tong tapped into his considerable potential and moved to our number two spot. Sophomore Andrew Adams, a 6'5" rookie with an affinity for liters of soft drinks, cracked into our front pack. Seniors Chris Shown, Dan Riherd, and Austin Swope and a couple of freshmen, Jon Richard and Lee Cunningham, gave us critical depth that would be invaluable as leg injuries would continue to be a tough opponent all fall.

Number three man Wes Aull was gimpy enough that we had to hold him out at the Tennessee Classic. Still, we had great effort throughout the lineup and finished second to always tough Memphis Houston, among the forty-six teams competing. Mark Rowe surged to the point at about 2,000 meters and never relinquished the lead, winning the tightly contested three miles in 15:30.

Mark had a super first half of the season. On the first weekend of October, at the Saluki Invitational on the campus of Southern Illinois University, Mark hit quick and very efficient splits of 5:01 and 9:59 on the way to 15:59 (5,000 meters), his sixth win in seven meets. We held off ever-improving Apollo, led by second place Isaac Lafond, 64–79.

Apollo threw down the gauntlet in our next two meetings. We won the Marshall County Invitational, besting the Eagles by 14 points, but Lafond beat Mark for the first time as they finished third and fourth, respectively.

With both running up near the front of the pack, it looked as if Isaac had Mark's number going into the regional as he again got the better of their dual at the Meet of Champions. St. Xavier and Louisville Male set the standard team-wise; we held off Apollo by a scant four points.

Regional

Fourth-ranked Apollo definitely came to the regional safari hunting for big game (Panther in particular). Coach Jeff Miller had them running with great confidence, and Isaac Lafond had established himself as the man to beat. Adding in the factor that the meet was to be held at Apollo's home course, lots of folks were predicting an Eagles victory as a huge throng invaded Ben Hawes State Park to watch the fireworks. Losing Andrew Adams to a stress factor, probably from a combination of the hard training surfaces and his love for caffeine, further complicated our task.

The demanding course began with two rolling loops before flattening out at about 2,500 meters. The fairly level reprieve lasted about 1,200 meters, then the trail reversed itself, and runners retraced their steps over one of the initial loops before finishing.

Patience is a virtue! Applying that advice to race strategy on this particular layout would be wise. Our plan was to be very smooth through the early, harsher terrain, attack the middle of the race and gut it out over the hills and turns of the last 600 meters.

One would think that Mark Rowe's confidence would have waned after his last two encounters against Lafond. If so, he sure didn't show it. Mark's pre-race question to me was, "At what point do I go?" My short,

simple reply relayed to Mark my belief that he would get the job done .
. ."You'll know!"

Mark's determination was furthered tempered by a couple of spectators that he dearly respected. One was Bob Puckett, my own high school
mentor and a legend in Kentucky cross country circles. Although he only
coached eight seasons back in the 60's and 70's, Coach Puckett's résumé
included five state champion and two state runner-up teams.

Sitting in a lawn chair near the starting hill was another long-time
cross country fan, my father-in-law, Bobby Henderson. Bobby loved to
watch the Panther teams and followed us from one end of Kentucky to
the other over the years. When his grandsons began to run, he became
even more endeared to the sport. Bobby, however, had been very ill for
several months following a series of small strokes and heart problems.
Mark desperately wanted to give his grandfather the gift of a special
effort on this day.

Runners rushed down the gentle hill off the starting line but quickly
calmed into a close pack, mindful of the ordeal ahead. At the end of the
first loop, our #2-#7 men were near the front of the chase pack.

Besides Mark and Lafond, Marshall County's Jeremy Burkeen had
joined the fray up front. Just beyond the mile point, they hit the steepest,
most significant incline in the race, stride for stride. Sensing the time was
right, Mark made his decisive move, bursting up the hill and opening up
about a ten yard lead over the top. The gap was stretched to 50 yards in
the flat section of the second mile. By the time he rounded the final turn
and began a short kick to the finish chute, Mark had an insurmountable
lead, breaking David Christian's old course mark with a 16:25 effort. Gift
delivered!

Burkeen held off Lafond for the runner-up honor. Looking out to
where the team race would be decided, I saw Apollo's fine senior, Kerry
Atherton, in the fourth position. Just yards behind him were three red
jerseys filled with Dan Riherd, Jon Richard, and Wes Aull, who all finished within two seconds of one another. Those three barely had time to
reach the end of the chute before Jordan Tong, Chris Shown, and Lee
Cunningham dashed in. Our men had constructed their finest hour of

Tony **Rowe**

the campaign with a 1–5–6–7–11–12–13 endeavor, turning back Apollo 30 to 52.

I was thrilled that Coach Puckett and my father-in-law, both of whom had a major impact on my life, were able to witness the competition. Bobby Henderson would have loved to have been in Lexington the following weekend but was not physically able to make the trip. Four months later . . . March 14, 2000 . . . he passed away. This was also the last cross country meet that Bob Puckett would ever witness. Coach was diagnosed with a quick-invading form of cancer, and on May 7th, he too was gone.

It's tough losing those you love, but memories are a blessing. I know that our family will carry with us those mental snapshots of a perfect October day for running in 1999, when . . . if just for a short time . . . cross country took us away from the tough circumstances of life as we shared some unique moments with special people . . . and all was good in our world.

State Meet '99

In what was supposed to be a rebuilding campaign, only two teams in Kentucky had beaten Daviess County going into the state meet. St. Xavier had been the pacesetter for teams across the state most of the fall and was the overwhelming choice to win in Lexington. Louisville Male, with six seniors in their seven man varsity lineup, had given us a pretty good licking, 119–145, at the Meet of Champions. In that meet our guys were somewhat impatient the first half of the 5,000 meters and faded the second half, certainly enabling the mature Male bunch.

The simple yet exciting pageantry of a Kentucky State Meet is special. The trees are trying to hang on to their multi-colored leaves. Pines (my favorite) are abundant in the area and add their green hue to the landscape. Often, you can see a flock of geese in their well-organized "V", headed south toward the warmer breezes. Add in the human effect of orange, blue, red, yellow, purple . . . in the form of team tents, sweats, uniforms, thousands of spectators . . . and you have an environment that is very unique. Adrenaline begins to flow even as you drive into the park. Controlling the extra "juice" and using it as an ally, rather than a liability, is critical to great performances. It could well be that this is the greatest coaching task surrounding the meet itself, and those who do it well always seem to come up with solid performances.

Being a team with little state meet experience, I knew our men would be more than a bit excited, and I did not want a repeat of the pacing mistake they made on this course two weeks prior. We were assigned a position near the middle of the starting line. The Pulaski County crew, with their fine senior, David Altmaier, was just a few boxes away. David was hoping to culminate an unbeaten season with a big performance.

Mark Rowe was very aggressive off the line, but after about 80 or 90 meters, he glanced to his left, and then began angling through runners until he was on Altmaier's shoulder. Mark apparently decided that if he had any chance of winning, he might as well challenge the favorite from the get-go. Our other six were smooth and patient. Mark chased Altmaier through the mile in 4:54 with the remainder of our scoring group around 5:20 to 5:25. Just past two kilometers, St. Xavier's talented freshman, Bobby Curtis, dropped Mark to the third position, pulling three others up with him. That trio included speedy James Doaty of Male, perhaps the premier prep half-miler in America.

The remainder of the Daviess County pack did not seem to be in a hurry with Tong, Aull, Richard, and Riherd all between 54th and 62nd. If they had any premium in their tanks, I was certainly ready to see it kick in . . . and indeed it did. Their collective effort over the final 2,500 meters was a piece of art. By two miles they had moved to 28–30–38 and 54 and we were within striking distance of Male; St. Xavier was well established in the lead.

In the final 400 meters Doaty picked up the third spot, and Brian Marr of Greenwood also slipped past Mark. Male's second man, David Wellerding, finished sixth. Our steady-paced performance paid off as Jordan Tong, who had struggled in the Meet of Champions and regional, ran 21st, one spot and one second ahead of Wes Aull. Just six seconds later, Dan Riherd came absolutely flying in. Dan, a tall (6'4") and strong athlete, concentrated on the 300 meter hurdles during track season. That speed paid off handsomely on this day as Dan picked off twenty-one people the final kilometer of the race, many of those coming in the last 400 meters. Also coming through with a big effort was freshman Jon Richard, who completed our scoring with a 43rd place effort. Fellow freshman Lee Cunningham ran a very commendable 56th and Chris Shown 60th.

St. X did not break from their early aggression and controlled the team race. Our men, however, not only caught Male, but opened a significant gap on the Bulldogs, 113–143; a 56 point swing from the Meet of Champions results. Jeff Miller's Apollo Eagles, led by Lafond (9th) and Atherton (14th), scored 149, resulting in both teams from our school system in the top four places.

An Excellent Decade

The 90's was an outstanding decade of cross country for our program. A sixth place, a fourth, a third, four runners-up, and three state championships made it a very fun ten years to be a Daviess County Panther. Six times during the decade we had the individual state champion. In '92, '94, '96, and '98 we had a Footlocker finalist, and the '98 team gained a #17 national ranking. As the 90's drew to a close and a new decade and century began, I wondered if we could sustain the success that had been generated in the very special previous ten years.

VI

— A New Century —

— 2000 —

I could really feel old knowing that my coaching career has touched four decades (70's-80's-90's-00's) and two centuries. (Think about it!) The freshness and clean slate of a new season, however, always helps put me in a youthful mood.

As a coach, there's always great anticipation before that first race. You can get a good feel for your squad and their potential, comparing workouts to past teams, but you really don't know until you jump into competition. For 2000, my expectations were high. We had seven seniors around for leadership, good potential in our sophomores and juniors, and an extremely talented freshman class.

The campaign began at our home course as we hosted the Daviess County Classic on my 46th birthday, and a solid team effort would be my present of choice. Since this was the season-opener, we wanted to give coaches the opportunity to see how their runners stacked up against one another, as well as against other teams. We had one race for each gender, allowing unlimited entries from each of the twenty schools on hand, making for a large, competitive field.

Our men exceeded my expectations. Mark Rowe opened his senior year with a 25 second victory, running 16:31 on a typically hot and muggy August morning. The improvement of all of our returnees was surprising. Senior Jordan Tong (4th), sophomore Jon Richard (6th), junior Andrew Adams (8th), hard-working senior Joe Collins (12th), senior Matt Anderson (16th), sophomore Lee Cunningham (18th) . . . I could not have asked for more . . . I got it anyway! Our freshmen showed they would have an impact in the years to come with Michael Cable (15th), Denny Weston (28th), Matt Rowe (39th), and Patrick Collier (48th) all besting every other team's fifth man. It was a red and white romp as the Panthers blitzed runner-up Greenwood 31–126.

Asked about his victory on my birthday, Mark explained to reporter Rich Suwanski, "I don't have any money, so this is the best I can do." Some things money cannot buy!

The Moon and the Son

We had just completed our second meet of the season, the Castle High School Invitational in Evansville, Indiana, and I pulled the bus into a parking lot behind a couple of fast food restaurants so the guys could fill their empty stomachs. My wife, Pam, and her mom were following behind us in a van. As I opened the door for the guys to unload, Pam pulled up beside us. She was furious!

"Somebody on the back of the bus just 'mooned' us."

"Everybody back on the bus," I hollered.

The team filed back to their seats and I assured Pam that the dastardly violator of women's innocence would be dealt with.

I let the team sit in silence for a moment and then asked, "Who mooned my wife?" After a few seconds one of the freshmen sheepishly confessed. I dismissed the rest of the squad to have a bit of one-on-one counseling with the young man. As the rest of the guys exited, several just shook their heads, trying to suppress an amused grin.

Meanwhile, Pam and Mrs. Henderson had gone into Burger King. As soon as some of the guys came in, Pam cornered them and asked, "So . . . who was it?" They delightfully responded, "Your son!"

That's how Matt kicked off his high school career. What Matt didn't know was that his cousin, Chelsea, and two other girls who attended our church were also riding in the van with Pam. Matt typified the freshman class. They were a competitive, energetic bunch who was not beyond pulling a good prank for the sake of entertainment. They knew what the limits were and didn't mind teetering right up to the edge, occasionally falling off.

About an hour and a half later, we were back at Daviess County High School. The rest of the team headed home as Matt headed for the football field to run 25 stadiums. Although a bit embarrassed by the episode, he was somewhat perplexed, "I thought mom would have recognized me!"

Good point!

The Season Rolls On

Our next outing was the South Oldham Invitational, and coach Houston Barber's host team was loaded. Their top man was someone we knew well. Isaac Lafond had transferred there from Apollo. Mark was feeling puny with a touch of strep throat. I should have held him out, but he was anxious to compete against Lafond again. You might think one early season meet would not have a huge impact on an entire season. Confidence, however, can be a fleeting sensation. The team in general and Mark, in particular, struggled through the hilly, twisting trail. Finishing ninth really deflated him, and it seemed Mark never completely regained the self-assurance he had at the Daviess County Classic. Although we were second overall, South Oldham flat dominated with Lafond the top medalist. What really bothered me was our lack of intensity. It was one of those meets that you leave thinking, "That wasn't any fun at all!"

After a sub-par performance, my tendency is to want to do what I can to remedy the situation . . . right away. That's why practice can be such a reprieve . . . and the next meet an opportunity for amnesty!

The first order of business on Monday . . . before the sweat began to pour . . . was a good tongue-lashing from me. Following a tough week of practice we wheeled into Nashville; the guys rolled through the three mile loop like the Chattanooga Choo-Choo! Mark ran 15:46, Jordan Tong 15:50, Andrew Adams 16:15, Joe Collins 16:31, and rapidly improving sophomore Jon Richard 16:34. We not only turned back Tennessee's #1 ranked squad, Knoxville Farragut, but also Hoover, Alabama, the most highly regarded team in the Heart of Dixie.

A couple of tough meets followed. After a twelve hour bus ride to Charlotte, North Carolina, we struggled through the Great American Cross Country Festival. Then, we were soundly thumped again by South Oldham, 32–94, at the Pike Central (Indiana) Invitational. It seems that teams often hit a plateau about the middle of the season. The anticipation and newness has worn off. The work has intensified and the guys need to take a collective deep breath before launching into the final weeks. This can be the critical point of the campaign. The athletes must decide if they will float through or refocus and turn it up a notch.

With our ego a bit deflated, the Panthers kicked off October at the City-County Meet. Mark and Jordan led all finishers, and we put fourteen runners in the top twenty. Then came a significant triumph over twenty-two other squads at Marshall County Invitational; among those teams was always-tough Louisville Trinity. An outstanding 23 point performance at the Logan County get-together preceded the final regular-season test, the thirty-six team Meet of Champions. Number one ranked South Oldham sat it out, but just about every other ranked team in Kentucky showed up at the Horse Park for this huge skirmish. Our guys were fit, race-sharpened and healthy, and I expected a terrific performance.

Cross country runners are tough. They spend months negotiating hundreds of miles over often rough terrain strewn with ditches, roots, molehills . . . when you think about it, one would expect a lot more foot and leg injuries than we see. After all that tough mileage, it would seem that walking 75 yards from our hotel to Fazoli's restaurant the night before the Meet of Champions would have been a breeze. Nope! A six inch high curb got the best of Jordan Tong, sidelining him with a twisted ankle. As a result, St. Xavier nudged us, 136–137; still, that loss was a definite confidence booster.

The competition for varsity spots throughout the fall was intense. Mark and Jordan led us. Andrew Adams and Jon Richard were both very steady, alternating in the #3 and #4 spots. It was not until late season that Lee Cunningham and Joe Collins nailed down their slots. The final varsity opening was a dogfight between Matt Anderson, sophomore Jared Keller, and three freshmen; Michael Cable, Matt Rowe, and Denny Weston. All had personal bests in the 17:30 to 17:50 range and took turns beating each other. As a coach, you sometimes just have to make tough decisions; however, you always hope the guys' performances will make your job easier. Michael Cable burst out of the mix with a strong run in the Meet of Champions, and our lineup for the championship season was finally set.

Regional

The 5,000 meter circuit at Keriakas Park in Bowling Green is basically two identical loops. The first half of each loop is fairly flat and fast, the second half rolling hills. Our top four went out very quick in the regional finals with Mark Rowe hitting a 4:50 first mile, Andrew Adams 4:53, Jon Richard 4:54, and Jordan Tong 4:56. Jordan seemed especially anxious to race after missing the previous meet. Before going to the starting line, he came to me, and with a little smile stated, "I've got something for you today!" I like that type of mindset. It not only tells me that a young man is confident in his fitness, but also that he is willing to work hard out on the course to assure success.

Bowling Green's Clay Pendleton, who spent the season both running and playing soccer, was well-prepared on his home course and opened a significant margin by the third mile. Late in the race Jordan caught Mark and out-legged him to the finish chute, delivering his pre-race promise; the two finished second and third. Adams (6th), Collins (10th), Richard (11th), Cunningham (13th), and Cable (17th) gave us plenty of reasons to smile as we outdistanced runner-up Bowling Green 32–97.

'00 State Meet

State meet is all about "turning it up" a notch. The idea is to run your best race of the year when it counts the most. That seed must be planted early, and we make our November expectations clear from the very beginning of summer practice. If we get beat by a more talented team, we can deal with it. If we don't give our very best effort, it is unacceptable. South Oldham proved they were Kentucky's best team on November 4th, but we certainly were at our finest.

Running conservatively early allowed our main pack to cover a lot of ground in a short period of time during the middle of the race and close with a flourish. Mark led the charge in eighth place, his fifth top 25 state finals finish. Jordan Tong earned an individual medal in fifteenth, while Andrew Adams (23rd), Jon Richard (32nd), and Lee Cunningham (46th) had very credible performances. I was extra pleased with the fact that our #6 and #7 men, Joe Collins and Michael Cable, both covered the 5,000 meters ahead of South Oldham's sixth man. Our 16:41 scoring average was actually faster than that of the '93 and '95 Panther teams that won the championship, and we carried home the silver trophy.

It's not every day folks get to see the turn of a century. Although I plan to be running on streets of gold 100 years from now . . . this was a great team to begin this current new era with.

Tony **Rowe**

— 2001 —

Kolby Knott was my captain in '01. He was the lone ranger . . . my only senior . . . one of the few guys we had with a driver's license. Behind him were three very talented classes, perhaps the premier back-to-back-to-back crew of my coaching career. Still, patience would be of essence with this bunch. With one more year of training, experience, and physical maturity, we could become a very dangerous team. Though young, our troop sent a strong message out across Kentucky on August 24th by putting seven men in the top 20 and turning back seventeen other teams in the Daviess County Classic.

That signal must have been interrupted somewhere in the airwaves between Owensboro and Louisville. Seven days after our meet, St. Xavier, running without their lead man, trounced us at the Warren East Invitational.

Those two meets set the pattern of our season. We dominated in our half of the state, winning significant invitationals at Apollo, Marshall County, and Logan County as well as our own 6k Relay. When we traveled east, the competition stiffened, giving us a clearer view of what to expect in November.

Sticks

There's an old saying something to the effect of "boys gotta have their toys." Even lots of grown men like to tinker with hot-rods, motorcycles, weapons . . . usually something that relates with power or release of aggression. I get a kick out of Tim "The Tool Man" Taylor on the show *Home Improvement*. He is an accurately portrayed stereotype of this unique male fixation on playthings.

The toy of choice for our '01 bunch, especially the younger ones, was sticks. There are lots of things guys can do with sticks . . . swing at rocks . . . sword fight . . . pole vault . . . the world just wouldn't be the same without 'em. At the Great American meet our team camp was under some nice shady trees. True to form, several of the guys retrieved some switches to help relieve their nervous energy and began to act out their best renditions of their favorite Ninja Turtles . . ."weapons" in hand. I was off doing my pre-meet thing, and when I returned some of our parents informed me that our guys had really insulted a lady. Observing their stick antics, she came over and gave them a tongue-lashing about tearing up trees, killing nature, and disrespecting the earth. (It takes all kinds!) Even though the trees didn't look any worse for the wear, I encouraged our guys to be respectful and they seemed to understand the need of leaving a little wood around for the sake of future generations. After the meet, as we were packing up, I noticed a very neatly organized plot of sticks they had "planted." Nothing like social consciousness!

We have a huge brown tarp that is used to stretch on at meets. At the Marshall County Invitational, we rolled it out in the middle of a wooded area. It was a cool, windy day and the freshman began gathering big, loose limbs. Within minutes they had constructed a very impressive tepee-like campfire, held together at the top by athletic tape. They assured me that they were not going to light it up, which was quite a relief considering the thick layer of dry leaves that covered the ground throughout the woods. Just looking at their finished product was enough to warm our spirits and inspire the team.

After the season, at our awards banquet, the freshmen gave me a plaque with a little stick pyramid glued to it, reminding me that . . . boys need their toys!

Team members warm up around their stick campfire
at the Marshall County Invitational.

Regional

The regional gathering at Madisonville proved to be a great test as Greenwood went out in a fast and furious pack. Before our guys seemed to recognize it, we had a lot of catching up to do. The scenario was an ironic flashback to the last time the regional championship was hosted on this same site. In '83, it was Madisonville that jumped out on us . . . the Panthers finally coming from behind to win. Now, 18 years later, we again entered the final mile in dire straits. Greenwood's #4 runner was right in the shadow of our #2 man. Finally, our guys reacted to the panic mode I was so vividly expressing, mixing well into the Greenwood pack in the final half mile. Talk about close! Over a 13 second span, the top four Panthers and Gators all slammed into the finish chute. Check out these results:

4.	Lee Cunningham	DC	17:21
5.	Kevin Dick	GW	17:22
6.	Michael Eaton	GW	17:26
7.	Jon Richard	DC	17:27
8.	Ian Sisson	GW	17:30
9.	Denny Weston	DC	17:31
10.	Brandon Berry	DC	17:31
11.	Jason Osborne	GW	17:34

Through four men each, the score was 30–30. Although Greenwood's fifth finisher was a very solid 17th, our remaining men, Michael Cable, Jared Keller, and Matt Rowe, raced in 13th, 14th, and 20th. We "pulled the fat out of the fire" with a 43–47 triumph.

State Meet '01

Lacking dominant front-runners, we depended on strong grouping and cautious pacing as allies at state. If anything, we were not aggressive enough. Our goal of hitting around 5:15 at the mile with our main group fell about five or six seconds short, and we were buried in the middle of the field; however, moments later we crossed under the "Kentucky State Championships" banner with our best #1-#5 gap of the season . . . 21 seconds. Sophomore Michael Cable led the tight Panther pack in 21st place. Within five seconds juniors Jonathan Richard (30th) and Lee Cunningham (31st) were in the corral. Sophomores Denny Weston (42ⁿᵈ) and Brandon Berry (44ᵗʰ) were never more than a couple of seconds apart, and our 145 point team score secured the third spot, behind St. Xavier and Shelby County.

Our young men made great strides (pardon the pun!) during the season, and with our entire varsity returning, the next fall couldn't get here fast enough.

— 2002 —

Our leader in 2002 was Jon Richard, David Christian's brother. If ever I have had a blue collar athlete, Jon was the man! Jon's parents, Mike and Donna, had been involved in our program since 1995 and became very close friends to Pam and me. For Jon's sake, as well as Mike and Donna's, I wanted to help find something that he could succeed in. As a seventh grader, being a bit too plump to be a distance runner, I encouraged Jon to begin throwing the discus for his middle school track team. Jon, however, wanted to run distance, and my urging him to throw seemed to be all the motivation he needed. Over the next year and a half Jon began to pile up the miles and drop the weight. You've heard the phrase, "I'm just an old lump of coal, but I'm gonna be a diamond someday!" That's a great description of Jon's transformation. By his senior year, Jon's work ethic and integrity was exactly what I was looking for in a team captain.

Beginning the season with your own invitational is great when the home team wins. We always get a huge crowd at the Daviess County Classic the last weekend of August. We have everybody from the cheerleaders to our principal and even our superintendent that come out and help us kick off the fall season. We have huge volunteer support from our parents, and the Classic truly is one of the highlight meets of our season. The weather is always hot and humid, and our course really tests the runners' summer training. It is mostly mildly rolling inclines and declines until the four kilometer mark, where a 200 meter hill we call "Goliath" greets the runners. About 200 meters later a smaller upgrade we have named "David" continues to test each athlete's fortitude. These two hills in themselves are not that tough, but where they lie within the course is the challenge; if Goliath doesn't get you . . . David will! More than once, a close team race has been broken open in this last kilometer of our meets.

Running well, especially through the middle and late stages of the race, we won our nineteen-team Classic, edging Louisville Trinity 39 to 54. A decent 37 second top five split hinted that we could be an excellent pack running squad by late season. The following weekend we went to the St. Xavier Invitational in Louisville. Despite the fact that our scorers averaged 16:41, we were spanked by South Oldham 75 to 95.

Brandon Berry (#3), Michael Hunter (#12), and Jon Richard (#18) work up "Goliath," just past the 4,000 meter mark in the 2002 Daviess County Classic.

Turning Point

Two weeks later, the Tennessee Classic was perhaps the most significant event in our season. Forty-seven teams and over 300 runners made this a mad dash over the steeplechase turf of Percy Warner Park. This is about the only flat ground in all of Nashville, and the course is the home of the Tennessee State Championships. Our guys ran solidly, but were clearly disgusted when the final results were tallied and Chattanooga McCallie squeaked by us 98 to 100. Later, I found out what happened on the cool-down jog after the awards ceremony. It would become a defining moment for our team. Halfway through their run, Jon Richard, Brandon Berry, Michael Hunter, Jared Keller, Drew Hawkins, Matt Rowe, and Denny Weston stopped for a little heart to heart talk. Each man decided he could have been the runner to make the difference in the outcome. They took the runner-up trophy and busted it into seven pieces. Each one put his piece of the trophy in his gym bag or locker as a commitment to each other that "we won't lose again!"

The Raging Red Line.

Blue Light Special

We have the greatest parents in the world supporting our program. One of them called me sometime before the Lexington Catholic Invitational and asked if I thought the team would like to stay in Lexington after the meet to watch the Kentucky-South Carolina football game. Well . . . is the Pope Catholic?!! I figured we could twist the guys' arms and persuade them to make the "sacrifice," and our friend purchased thirty tickets for the team. The game itself was a neat experience for the squad, many of whom had never seen a big-time college contest. It was especially entertaining to watch South Carolina coach Lou Holtz pace the sideline. I would estimate he covered about five miles, 30 yard line to 30 yard line, back and forth, walking, hollering, "helping" the officials, strategizing. The guy has great endurance. Maybe he should have been in our sport.

It was late night as we departed Big Blue country, and before long most of the guys were snoozing. After being on the road for about two hours, somewhere close to midnight, we found ourselves on a dark, lonely stretch of the Western Kentucky Parkway. Suddenly, a blue light flashed behind us and our bus driver, Ron Towery, lamented, "He got me!"

Sitting near the front of the bus, I asked, "For what?"

"Speeding . . . I was going 62 miles per hour."

I told Ron I didn't think the trooper would have pulled him over for going that speed, but Ron, visibly shaken, was already nervously pulling out his driver's license as he pulled the bus off the road and opened the door. Figuring that I didn't have a dog in this fight, I leaned back and was ready to resume a little nap. The officer stepped onto the bus and in the dark I heard him say, "No, no . . . I don't need your license. Is Coach Rowe on the bus?" I sat back up and the trooper said, "Hey Coach . . . did ya'll win today?" It was Neal Pagan, a Kentucky state patrolman that had run for me a few years earlier. Knowing it was cross country season, seeing Daviess County on the side of the bus from when we passed his position and remembering that I usually drove these trips, Neal figured he would use his authority to get a little prank in and say hello. After chatting a few moments, we were back on the road. Ron Towery, who took great pride in doing everything by the book, was still a bit traumatized, albeit relieved. I loved it!

The team cools off after the 2002 Lexington Catholic Invitational.

A significant development for us was the improvement of sophomore Trae Gaddis from meet to meet. One week before the regional, at the Metro Meet of Champions on the St. Xavier course, Trae was our fifth man, running 16:39. He had run 17:37 there the second week of the season.

Another reason for optimism was the progression of our scoring pack running closer to one another. At the Lexington Catholic Invitational and Meet of Champions, we put up #1-#5 man splits of 29 and 25 seconds and were well prepared for the regional in Marshall County.

At the regional, junior Brandon Berry (2nd-16:37) led another tight pack of 27 seconds through our top five and 36 seconds for all seven men. Senior Michael Hunter (5th-16:48), senior Jon Richard (6th-16:51), sophomore Drew Hawkins (9th-16:56), senior Jared Keller (12th-17:04), junior Matt Rowe (14th-17:13), and Trae Gaddis (15th-17:13) completed an outstanding effort, and we were headed for the Horse Park.

'02 State Championship–A Lesson in Packing

We had not seen #1 ranked South Oldham since the St. Xavier Invitational the second week of the season. They dominated in Kentucky throughout the fall and were highly favored to take home the big trophy at state. Championships, however, are not won on paper. As they say in rodeo circles, "ain't no horse can't be rode . . . ain't no cowboy can't be throwed!" Translation? We had a shot!

Race day saw good weather conditions, and the pace was hot. Hunter and Richard hit the mile mark in 5:03, Berry 5:04, Keller 5:06, and Gaddis 5:09, with Hawkins and Rowe in tow. South Oldham's top two were ahead of our group, but their #3-#7 guys began to reveal a small chink in their armor. We stayed in our rubber band (stretch but don't break) pack, and our top five all pressed through two miles between 10:20 and 10:28. I was getting excited! I made sure every one of our guys knew we were taking the rest of the field to task, and they responded with a great last mile. Michael Hunter (9th) and Jon Richard (10th) led our charge to the finish with less than a second separating them. Berry (14th), the late-blooming Gaddis (22nd), and Keller (23rd) closed out our scoring. Our 20 second spread was the best we had run all season. Knowing the results were going to be close, we gathered around a camcorder, looking at a video of the race that one of our parents had taken. Carefully counting the places we began to celebrate. The official results later revealed that we had upset favored South Oldham by 25 points.

From the Tennessee Classic our young men had gone on a single-minded mission. They were true to their promise not to lose again, finishing with a stellar 209–2 record. Even after graduation, many of that group of seven has his piece of the trophy that was busted up on their cool-down that day in Nashville. Their collective, golden state championship hardware sits predominantly in the center trophy case at Daviess County High School.

(l. to r.) Jay Barron, Jon Richard, and Matt Rowe leave their mark on the 2002 state championship trophy.

An "Eggcellent" Celebration

Everyone has his own way of celebrating victory. This team was unique! On the bus ride home from Lexington late Saturday evening, they decided to meet at Brandon Berry's home about 11:00 p.m. Brandon lived out in the county, and the team would often go to his house for a bonfire, four-wheeling, "cow tipping," or whatever entertainment they could create. On the way to Brandon's, a bunch of them stopped by Wal-Mart and purchased about 12 dozen eggs. It just so happened a local policeman was near them in the checkout area. As you might imagine, the officer was more than a little interested in what the guys intended to do with all those eggs. He had doubts they were planning a breakfast! The boys assured this fellow they were true, blue supporters of truth, justice and the American way and invited him to Brandon's for an innocent egg fight, celebrating their championship. Somehow, the officer bought into their innocence, and the celebration was on. True to their word, the only victims of flying egg yoke that night was one another . . . and maybe a few cows!

— 2003 —

"Now this is the law of the jungle–as old and as true as the sky -
And the wolf that shall keep it will prosper–but
the wolf that shall break it will die–
As the creeper that girdles the tree trunk - the
law runneth forward and back-
For the strength of the pack is the wolf–and
the strength of the wolf is the pack!
-Unknown-

Cross country is a "contact" sport! It is all about pack running. Sometimes, similar abilities allow natural team packing. More often than not, however, coaches must teach and preach packing in workouts and meets. From early on, our '03 team had good grouping and great depth, creating lots of competition for varsity spots.

Opening with the Daviess County Classic, we crammed ten men into the top 33 spots, and we felt pretty doggone good about ourselves. Visions of back to back championships were dancing in our heads. The next couple of weeks brought us quickly back down to earth. Just after the Classic, my son Matt, who had experience in two state meets, had a tonsillectomy, and his activity would be greatly limited for the next three weeks. Still, we went to the very competitive St. Xavier Invitational on the second weekend of the season expecting great results.

As the race at Seneca Park unfolded, Brandon Berry, Trae Gaddis, Josh Yeckering, Jon Dunaway, Drew Hawkins, Tyler Stanley, and Denny Weston were running strong and well-packed. About two miles into the race, Brandon Berry pulled ahead of our group and went around a bushy turn on the course. It was marked with a long metal rod with a directional flag on top. The runner ahead of Brandon pulled on the pole as he rounded the turn and left it leaning out toward the running path. As Brandon negotiated the corner a couple of seconds later, the top of the rod caught him just under the rib cage, scraped up under his arm, and tore a hole through the back of his jersey. Brandon, needless to say, was writhing in pain. When our pack came through the turn and saw their leader lying on the ground in agony, they fell apart. Brandon, of course, was unable to finish the race. He was severely hurting for several minutes and sore for a few days, but we were thankful that he had not been impaled. That incident caused state officials to take a serious look at how courses were marked. In the final standings, we finished fifth, 62 points behind champion St. Xavier.

Anxious to put that meet behind us, we jumped into an aggressive week of training. On a recovery day during the middle of the week, about nine guys made a corporate decision to take about 800 meters off of a scheduled seven miler, cutting short the middle of the route. Now . . . integrity is a word our team hears often from me. My definition of integrity is "doing the right thing even if no one is watching." As a coach, you may not be able to force reliability and honesty, but you can certainly enforce your regulations and hope that sooner or later the guys will catch on. Over the course of the season, a half mile is not going to make a physical difference in fitness. Lack of responsibility and upright behavior, however, can be infectious and destroy a team.

The following morning we were scheduled for a 6:30 am five miler at school. When the guys got there, I told them to report to the track. They circled the oval twenty times that morning, twenty-four times in the afternoon, and twenty times the next morning as I tallied each lap on paper. I held the naughty nine out of the next meet, putting them through a time trial instead. Message received, we had no more problems during the fall with self-imposed, shortened workouts. Still yet, the entire first month seemed to be a struggle, and I began to wonder if this group had what it took to achieve elusive back to back State titles.

Question Answered

On September 30th, the City-County Championships were contested at Yellow Creek Park. Brandon Berry paced the field through the first mile in 5:08. Six seconds behind him were half a dozen red-clad teammates. Two miles later, a victorious Berry led the Panther parade with Josh Yeckering (3rd), Jon Dunaway (4th), Drew Hawkins (5th), a recovering Matt Rowe (6th), Josh Lockhart (7th), and Brett Schrooten (9th). Interestingly, although Schrooten never made our state meet seven in cross country, Brett won two state titles in the 100 meters on the track.

The City-County effort marked a turning point in our season. Putting the injuries and struggles behind, our guys improved and gained confidence with every race. At the Lexington Catholic Invitational we finished runner-up to St. Xavier, 65–73 and rode that momentum into the Metro Meet of Champions in late October on their home course. Averaging 16:30, we actually tied the Tigers, 47–47. The tiebreaker (first 6th man across the line), gave them the win, but I believe we gained the psychological advantage that day, making huge strides since the second week of the season on the same course.

Matt Rowe prepares to race.

We rolled through the regional, placing our five scorers in the top eight and set up what looked to be one of the fiercest championship battles in years. The Kentucky Track and Cross Country Coaches Association played the scenario up big in its pre-state press release. It read like this:

> . . . watch out for the fireworks . . . Daviess County has literally been chasing St. Xavier all over the state this season. How big a gap is there? At the Metro Meet of Champions using raw scores as the meet scoring system, St. Xavier won on the sixth man tiebreaker. The regional/state meet scoring system would have had Daviess County a one point winner. That close. Over the last ten years Daviess County has won four titles and St. Xavier three. Check out the starting line before watching the race to see if Chuck Medley has St. X wearing green, gold or its "forest green at night" black so you can tell who contenders are. Look for the red and white Panthers and the St. Xavier color-of-choice . . . count every single point and place exchange on the course. By 3:17 Saturday, the verdict will be known.

The "color of choice" part of the preview was amusing to us since we had already decided to pull out some black uniforms for the weekend. It really didn't matter what color other teams were wearing. I want my guys to glance at the other teams and have an idea about what is going on, but mostly concentrate on each other and our own plan. Why overload the psyche? Our job is to run a great team race and let the result take care of itself.

2003 State Championship—The Pack Attack

I told someone before the race that I would gladly take a one point victory, and the prognostication of a close race held absolutely true, although the principals, as they say in boxing, were slightly different. The self-assurance and belief in one another that our men had acquired over the last six or seven meets shone brilliantly. They say a team is as strong as its weakest link. We had none! At the mile, seniors Josh Yeckering, Brandon Berry, Matt Rowe, juniors Tyler Stanley, Trae Gaddis, Drew Hawkins, and sophomore Jon Dunaway presented a basically impenetrable unit, all passing through between 5:06 and 5:12. My heart was pumping like crazy! The adrenaline a state meet generates is amazing. A clearly visible determination could be read on each face and in the body language of our young men as they passed by again one half mile later. The farther we got into the race, the more excited I became, and I made sure the team knew it. When they see that type of emotion from me, they know something special is going on, and tend to feed off of it, picking up their intensity. St. Xavier had chosen to wear gold uniforms, but for whatever reason, they were not up to par. We were still very well grouped at two miles with a 10 second spread through our scorers. Moments later, as the pack flew through the long tunnel of fans that lined the path to the finish, the outcome seemed to be clear. Each of our runners impacted the team score as all seven men finished ahead every other teams' fifth.

Emotion

I am so thankful to be in the position to impact young lives, and having the opportunity to coach my own sons has been a double blessing. One moment that will stick with me is that of my youngest son Matt crossing the finish line, the seventh man of a packed Daviess County team (:32 #1-#7 split), pumping his fist into the air, jubilant with the performance of the team. When I got to the chute area he was beaming. A few seconds later he was literally crying, filled with the emotions of knowing this would be his last state meet, the joy of victory, the relief, and who knows what else. It was a neat scene! Cross country affords the opportunity for so many young people to learn so much about themselves.

Wow! That Was Close!

Knowing that we had turned back the challenges of St. Xavier and Trinity, the hugs, high fives and celebration was on as our guys exited the roped-off chute. Moments later someone asked, "What about Greenwood?" The question caught me by surprise. We had handily beaten Art Sciubba's team the previous week in the regional. I had barely noticed them during the race. After a few anxious moments, self-appointed investigator Denny Weston came up and exclaimed, "It's official; we beat Greenwood by two points." Whew! The guys had delivered that one point win I said I would be happy to see . . . with a point to spare!

"For the strength of the pack is the wolf-and the strength of the wolf is the pack!"

The 2003 squad celebrates the 2nd of three consecutive state championships.

Coaching Your Sons

There is a verse in Proverbs 22:6 that reads, "Train up a child in the way he should go: and when he is old, he will not depart from it." Many people interpret this as a scripture about disciplining your kids. However, I heard a theologian teach that this verse also speaks of encouraging your children toward their own unique interests, characteristics, and gifts. Give them the opportunities to thrive in the areas they are most satisfied with and let them be comfortable in their own skin.

While not always the case, still, many coaches' children will gain an interest in the same sport their father or mother is involved in. Growing up around that activity often allows the children unique and accelerated insights and understanding of the particular sport. Often, coaches' children have advanced skill levels because they have tagged along to the field, gym, or track from early on.

I have had the unique privilege of being both father and coach to each of my sons. I am a family man. From the time they were young, I hoped (maybe even secretly prayed) both Mark and Matt would run for me. Still, I had to let each one choose.

From the time he was young, Mark had an extraordinary interest in my track and cross country teams. Being born a two-pounder, he was always wiry. We knew from early on that Mark would be a runner. Matt, on the other hand, had a great variety of athletic interests. He had a bit more meat on his bones, so to speak, than Mark. However, between his sixth and eighth grade years, Matt really slimmed and gained a lean runner's physique. Pam and I tried to keep an open mind to our sons' interests, but we were obviously excited when each chose to concentrate on running. For eight straight years (1996–2003) one or both of them donned a Daviess County High School jersey.

Perhaps the greatest single reward in coaching my sons was the extra time I was able to spend with them. I have heard that the average father in America spends less than one minute each day in meaningful communication with their children. Unbelievable! How can a man pass his values on to his children with such a pitiful investment in their lives? Deuteronomy 6:7 speaks of passing on Godly values. It says, "You shall teach them diligently to your children, and shall talk of them when you sit in your house, when you walk by the way, when you lie down, and when you rise up." Some of the more meaningful times and conversations I have had with Mark and Matt have been on runs through the trails, over the hills, and down the roads together.

Coaching them also helped me become more considerate of all my athletes' needs. With large teams, I have several runners each day with aches, pains, and injuries. It is easy to get a bit insensitive to their complaints and shrug them off. When Mark and Matt began running for me and had setbacks, the coach in me said, "Run through it," but the father in me said, "Maybe we need to back down a bit in our training." Now I tend to listen more to the concerns of all my athletes.

One great apprehension surrounding coaching your children is fairness. Pressure comes with the territory. Being a coach's kid is akin to being a preacher's kid. They are expected to walk a somewhat finer line and make less mistakes and that tends to add an element of anxiety that other athletes may not feel.

For me, being fair to my sons was more an issue of not putting unnecessary pressure on them. I wanted to let them know that my love for them was unconditional and not tied into their accomplishments as runners. I tried to make a conscientious effort not to talk too much about running at home. Reflecting on his time under my tutelage, Mark stated, "when we were at practice you were my coach but when we were home you were my dad . . . if the line was crossed it was usually because I brought it up."

Practice and competition, however, was a different story. A coach tends to take everything a bit more personally when their child is involved. I expected so much out of Mark and Matt that I sometimes found myself being critical of their practice or race performance before talking to them. Usually, there was a valid reason for what may have looked like a lesser effort. What I finally learned was that both my sons desperately wanted to please me.

Then there's the matter of playing time. When a coach inserts his own son or daughter into the lineup, he will either look like a genius or a goat, depending on the performance of the child. That opens the coach to the ire of parents whose youngsters are sitting on the bench. With running, it is less subjective. If you beat someone to the finish line, it is hard to argue the result.

The bottom line for my family was that we were able to share some very special moments with each other. Meets became family trips. Team championships became more personal. At one point Mark was a senior and Matt was a freshman as teammates on the same Daviess County squad. I really believe that both of them thoroughly enjoyed their time in our program and respected my position as their coach. As a matter of fact, Matt summed it up from a very unique perspective, "We saw how much you loved it. To have the satisfaction of *you* knowing that we also enjoyed it was very rewarding for us."

— 2004 —

A Nice Surprise

In the fall of 2003, I was asked by the Kentucky High School Coaches Association to fill out a questionnaire in consideration for regional and national coaching honors. Weeks later I received word that I was one of eight national finalists for boys cross country coach of the year. The awards ceremony was to be held in Las Vegas in the summer of '04. Pam and I had never been to this oasis in the desert, and the idea of meeting and learning from some great coaches throughout the United States was a unique opportunity. Our school backed the venture, and in late June we were on our way.

Now . . . while there is no place of complete virtue and innocence in our world . . . there is a huge contrast between Owensboro, Kentucky and Las Vegas. Maybe I just don't get out much! Our feet had barely touched the ground at the airport when evidences that we were in "Sin City" began to materialize. We won't get into that . . . but . . . whew!

The sights in Las Vegas are quite spectacular, and the convention was both educational and inspiring. All of the cross country finalists (eight boys' coaches and eight girls' coaches) met together and presented sessions about their programs. I felt honored to meet and learn from great coaches like Forry Flaagan, head of the outstanding Stevens, South Dakota program, and Pete Moss, the long-time coach at Benzie County Central in Michigan, who had 47 years of coaching excellence. There was Harvey Honyouti and Rickey Baker, who teamed as girls and boys coaches at Hopi High School in Arizona. They have taken so many young, underprivileged Native Americans, instilled hope and pride, and transformed them into champions! I left those meetings both stimulated and challenged!

On the evening of the awards banquet, seventeen different National Coach of the Year awards were presented in the various sports. It was quite an honor sitting in front of the room with the other seven finalists in our sport as the master of ceremonies introduced each of us to the audience, reviewing our careers. Then came the announcement, "The boys cross country National Coach of the Year . . . from the Bluegrass State. . . . I like to have fallen out of my chair!

Pam made a few phone calls to some excited folks back home. It was amusing to see Mark and Matt's reactions to the award. Mark, the ever-believing one was ecstatic and told Pam, "I knew dad would get it!" Matt was equally excited and later put things in perspective in his own witty way, "It didn't surprise me dad won . . . after all . . . he had a one out of eight chance."

After the ceremony, Pam and I decided to celebrate in a big-time way. We went to a Denny's restaurant just down from Harrah's, where we were staying, and ordered two hot-fudge brownie delights. We gobbled those suckers down, relishing every last chocolate calorie . . . laughing the entire time . . . and agreed we would not even feel guilty! After all, as they say . . ."what happens in Vegas, stays in Vegas!"

In truth, no one accomplishes anything by himself. Coaching honors are representative of the sweat, sacrifice, and support of lots of folks: athletes, parents, administrators. It was a thrill to win National Coach of the Year, but it was definitely the result of a team effort. Getting back home and sharing the award was perhaps the best part of our entire experience.   Perspective is everything. Perhaps, in athletics, because we are in the public eye, we tend to get an over exaggerated opinion of ourselves. In America, we have farmers, coal miners, construction workers, secretaries . . . that faithfully carry out their responsibilities . . . without the hype . . . day after day. They are the ones stories should be written about. They are the heart and soul of our country.

Nevertheless, the National High School Athletic Coaches Association allowed us an experience we will never forget. The award itself was very humbling and made me realize what an extraordinary situation I have had through the years at Daviess County High School. I have indeed been very, very blessed!

Tony and Pam Rowe at the National High School Athletic
Coaches Association banquet in the summer of 2004.

On with the Good Stuff

They say that getting to the top is not as tough as staying at the top! It took all of about 17 minutes into the '04 season to confirm that. St. Xavier came down to Owensboro for the first time in years and trounced us in the season-opening Daviess County Classic, 45–99. Seven days later, in their invitational, the Tigers were 62 points better than us. Our two teams went head-to-head twice more during the regular season with St. Xavier giving us two more solid whippings, 56–136 at Greenwood, and 51–103 at the Horse Park on October 2nd.

We needed a confidence booster in a big-time way. As in '03, the City-County Meet served as a pivotal event in our campaign. Senior Drew Hawkins won his second meet of the year at Ben Hawes Park, where Apollo hosted the competition. Tyler Stanley, Nathan Malony, Jon Dunaway, and Trae Gaddis were second through fifth to make it a clean sweep and a perfect score of 15 points. Two weeks later we handled eventual class AA state champion Paducah Tilghman at the Marshall County Invitational.

On November 6th, at Logan County, our guys were very sharp. With all five scorers in the top 11 spots, the Panthers hoisted the regional championship trophy for the 10th consecutive year. The question now was how to beat a very talented St. Xavier squad, a feat no team in Kentucky had accomplished this season.

The Panther pack is solid 600 meters into the 2004 Apollo Invitational.

Say Something—Anything!

Trae Gaddis was one of those guys who just naturally stayed fit through the years because he was about half hyper. He didn't always put the summer miles in that I would like to have seen; however, by the end of each season Trae would round into shape, and we could count on his best effort. From the time we boarded the bus at noon on Friday before state, Trae was scary quiet. I didn't quite know what to think. Trae had an outgoing personality, to say the least. Since he didn't seem to be suffering from the effects of any observable illness, I assumed maybe Trae was just concentrating on this, his final high school cross country race. Time would tell!

We were about to go to battle with perhaps our oldest team ever at state. Trae and fellow seniors Tyler Stanley, Drew Hawkins, Nathan Malony, Wes Mobley, and Josh Lockhart, along with junior Jon Dunaway would be the ones to try and defend our state title and make history. Since the reclassification of schools in 1980, no class AAA (large school) program in Kentucky had ever accomplished a three-peat. Having had a hand in two state championships already, this group could easily have embraced that success and perhaps be mentally complacent, relieving themselves of the pressure that was clearly on their shoulders. However, that's not what champions are about. Rather, it seemed they were putting even more expectations on themselves. Hopefully, that's what precipitated Trae's uncharacteristic demeanor. Like the two previous years, we were not favored to win, but also like the '02 and '03 teams, this group did not want second place!

Arriving at the Horse Park that evening, we found a very sloppy course from a wet week leading up to the meet. I told the team that the mud would be to our advantage because we had some big, strong guys who could plow through it.

Race day was rain free with a good breeze, but there was no way the course would be dry by race time. As a matter of fact, with the girls and boys class A and AA races preceding ours, it was a good bet that the course would be even more deteriorated by the time we ran. We went through our normal state meet routine, including having the Lord's Prayer with the team, our parents, and our fans, before we sent the guys off to the starting line. This is a tradition that began somewhere in the mid-90's, and it seems to really give the team a lift. Dozens of people bowing their heads together and reciting that beautiful prayer and then breaking the huddle to their cheers imputes strength that I really believe our guys can feel.

I met with the team one final time after they ran strides, just moments before race time. Generally, I am not a real "rah-rah" type guy in the team huddle. I feel like those last minute fiery pep talks wear off by about two minutes into the race. I prefer to remind the guys of their race plan and let them save the mental energy for when it will be needed. For some reason, however, I became very animated about us getting this thing done, to the point that some of the guys seemed to be caught off guard. I then headed across the creek and up the hill to the top side of the course as our team reported to the line.

Race Plan—What Race Plan?

I always position myself somewhere near the 800 meter mark at the Horse Park, waiting for the pack to pass by the first time. I expected our guys to be well grouped around 40th or 50th place when they came into view and moving up well. What I actually saw both excited and scared me! Dunaway, Hawkins, and Stanley had already charged into the top ten spots, and the rest of our pack was close behind. Addressing myself, I audibly heard the words, "I hope they can hold on!" We were clearly in the lead, and we had clearly abandoned the conservative race plan we had set up. With all caution thrown to the wind, now we were going to have to win it the hard way; keep attacking and ignore the pain.

We did just that and surprisingly, at the mile mark, no other team seemed to have closed on us much. Stanley was in about sixth place, and we had a pack of five guys about ten seconds behind him. I knew if we could get about halfway through the race in good shape that the excitement of the crowd lining the creek area, the adrenaline and the sloppy course would make it hard for anyone to come back on us. At about one and a half miles I began yelling to our guys that we were going to make history. Pre-race favorite St. Xavier seemed to be struggling and had their hands full with their rival, Louisville Trinity. Another half mile passed, and I was literally pinching myself to make sure this wasn't a dream. Rarely had I seen a team on such a mission as our squad. Late in the race, we began to pay for our hot early pace, but we never broke. Stanley crossed the finish line in eighth place, Hawkins 13th, Dunaway 18th, Malony 25th, and a jubilant Trae Gaddis 30th. He was quiet no more! It is a special feeling to know that the issue has been settled as your fifth man sprints in . . . and this one was never in doubt! The final tally showed our guys had raced to Daviess County's ninth state title and the unprecedented three-peat. Trinity held off St. Xavier for second 116 to 127, but our low score of 81 was golden. It was time to bite another trophy!

— 2005 —

Replacing six of your top seven runners is a task, yet that was our challenge as the '05 season got underway. We did return a number of juniors and seniors without varsity experience and inherited an excellent freshman class. Two more additions, talented juniors Jordan Clark and Jordan Payne, made our rebuilding project a bit easier. Clark had great success as an eighth grader, but had not been involved in our sport since. Payne was a Daviess County native whose family had lived in the Marshall County area for a number of years and moved back home.

Developing confidence in varsity situations would be critical to success, and we approached that chore with aggressive pre-season training and one of the toughest schedules in school history. We opened the fall with a rather unimpressive debut at our own Classic. Louisville Trinity and Lexington Dunbar relegated us to third place. On the positive side, our junior varsity captured nine of the top 10 spots in their division of the meet. The next five weeks resulted in two invitational wins (Madisonville and Greenwood) and three lessons in running (Memphis Twilight Classic, Tennessee Classic and Jesse Owens Classic), where some of Dixie's best teams exposed our weaknesses. The lack of frontrunners kept our team scores high.

It was not until October 4th that I came away from a meet satisfied. Jon Dunaway, our only returnee with state meet experience, turned back a tough local field in the City-County Championships. Payne, Clark, surprising Benji Whitehead, and always steady Brad Horn gave us five finishers in the top nine. We turned back eventual Class AA state champions, Owensboro Catholic, by a 27–52 margin, and seventeen of our men ran seasonal personal bests.

It's good to head into the post-season on a high note. At the Christian County Invitational we ran without two of our top five. Jon Dunaway was taking the ACT, and Brad Horn was nursing a nagging leg injury. Regardless, we averaged 17:18 through five men and turned back eighteen other squads. Horn, our ultimate pacesetter, was still limping around a week later and would be unavailable the balance of the season. Our late-season lineup would consist of seniors Jon Dunaway and Ryan Cravens, juniors Jordan Clark, Jordan Payne, Benji Whitehead, and Shane Powell, and freshman Wes Russelburg.

A Warm Regional

The regional championships were contested on a sunny, breezy day at Phil Moore Park in Bowling Green. The 80 degree November weather extended what had been a very warm season. Two of our guys suffered heat problems late in the competition, but all seven were across the line before second place Calloway County's third man. For the 11th year in a row, the Raging Red Line reigned as kings of the region.

Though we had a solid second half of the season, it seemed that we still were not "hitting on all eight cylinders." Our final tough workout of the season took place on Monday, five days before state. The session called for 2 x 1 mile on the road . . . full blast in race shoes. That first mile told me what I wanted to know. Jon Dunaway ran 4:27, Powell 4:29, Payne 4:33, Clark 4:38, Cravens 4:42, Whitehead 4:43, and Russelburg 4:46. Finally, I knew we were physically capable of a big effort and the time was right.

Tony **Rowe**

State Meet '05

Physical capabilities must be tempered by emotional readiness to reach the desired November pinnacle. Coaching, like life itself, is such a challenge. Don't ever assume you've got it all figured out. There are so many variables in athletics; training, injuries, team dynamics, dependence upon individuals to become one unit . . . you just can never take for granted you have "arrived." Before this season, we had only finished out of the top three at state once since 1991.

State meet did not go well for us. The plan was to pack well and try to be in a certain range of places at different points of the race. Our guys lost contact with one another shortly off the line, seemed to panic, and never regrouped. Maybe the pressure of defending three straight state titles was more than they were ready for. Perhaps it was inexperience . . . possibly something I missed in preparing them. Jordan Payne (27th), Benji Whitehead (52nd), and Wes Russelburg (53rd) had credible efforts, but their four teammates really struggled. While seventh place is not what we had envisioned . . . still . . . that's what we got! On the positive side, five guys that will return in '06 gained valuable experience.

There were some long faces on the bus ride back to Western Kentucky. Almost home . . . we passed the road sign that read "Daviess County." Crossing that line seems to always have a certain effect on me that is hard to explain. A few years ago, an area newspaper ran a story about our program and led the article off with the line . . ." Daviess County is running country." I like that! If . . . through the decades . . . the performance of our athletes has added an unassuming pride to the folks along our stretch of the river . . . then I can't wait to get out there and do it all again next year. I love this sport!

Daviess County at State Since 1977

Note: In the state meet, those runners competing as individuals are removed from computations of scoring in determining the team champion. Therefore, our total scores listed here are lower than the sum of our top five finishers in each race.

*Team state champion   **Individual state champion

	1977			1978	
2	McKay Mattingly	10:01	1	McKay Mattingly**	15:23
7	Scott Eckstein	10:22	11	Scott Eckstein	16:03
33	Mike Rhodes	10:56	12	Mike Rhodes	16:05
61	Brian Autry	11:13	49	George Weatherholt	16:59
65	George Weatherholt	11:17	51	John Dickinson	17:01
	Team Score	118		Team Score	97
	Team Place	3rd		Team Place	2nd
85	Sam Wilson	11:36	52	Mike Linville	17:03
112	Joel Ray	11:59	53	Jerry Weihe	17:03
	1979			1980	
5	Mike Rhodes	16:49	91	Jeff O'Bryan	18:33
22	Jerry Weihe	17:20			
29	Brian Autry	17:29			
35	Gregg Smith	17:37			
73	Jimmy Evans	18:10			
	Team Score	124			
	Team Place	2nd			
109	Tim Frost	18:33			
117	Dennis Brown				
	1981			1982*	
21	Scott Katchuk	17:15	4	Scott Katchuk	16:40
49	Dennis Brown	17:45	14	David Douglas	17:06
60	Darren Christian	17:57	17	Dennis Brown	17:10
63	Richard Bowen	17:59	26	Rich Bowen	17:21
67	Dean Roberts	18:01	27	Dean Roberts	17:22
	Team Score	204		Team Score	59
	Team Place	6th		Team Place	1st
87	Dane Allen	18:16	37	Darren Christian	17:33
89	Kevin Marsch	18:20	40	Kevin Clark	17:36
	1983			1984	
13	Dean Roberts	17:06	18	Bill Dechman	17:10
23	Bill Dechman	17:26	29	Tom Dycus	17:39
25	Kevin Clark	17:28	31	Steve Payne	17:40
54	Tom Dycus	17:53	51	Kenny Linville	18:02
61	Kenny Linville	18:00	73	Paul Warrenfeltz	18:22
	Team Score	146		Team Score	162
	Team Place	3rd		Team Place	4th
69	Tony Stinnett	18:09	85	Troy Adkins	18:37
70	Steve Payne	18:10	102	Rodney Bivins	19:03

	1985				1986	
15	Paul Warrenfeltz	16:56		11	Mark Stuart	16:44
22	Mark Stuart	17:06		15	Paul Tedenby	17:00
29	Gustaf Mark	17:17		22	Paul Warrenfeltz	17:07
50	Troy Adkins	17:37		31	Steve Gilbert	17:22
53	Robert Bivins	17:38		68	Troy Adkins	18:03
	Team Score	130			Team Score	115
	Team Place	3rd			Team Place	2nd
81	Jimmy Vanover	18:12		101	Richard Howard	18:43
83	Steve Gilbert	18:13		112	Jon Locher	19:10

	1987				1988	
2	Mark Stuart	16:07		6	Bob Foster	16:39
40	Neal Anderson	17:36		17	Neal Anderson	17:10
58	Robert Murley	17:52		18	Steve Gilbert	17:12
71	Richard Howard	17:59		22	Robert Murley	17:14
80	Jon Locher	18:06		42	Mike Bruner	17:40
	Team Score	205			Team Score	99
	Team Place	8th			Team Place	3rd
103	Troy Adkins	18:40		75	Mike Claycomb	18:13
106	Mike Claycomb	18:43		81	Chris Goodman	18:16

	1989				1990	
3	Bob Foster	16:38		3	Bob Foster	16:36
49	Brian Clark	17:54		28	Steve Bair	17:39
73	Mike Bruner	18:11		51	Mark Lattin	18:13
78	Jason Clark	18:18		67	Jason Clark	18:30
				76	Jeremy Kruger	18:42
					Team Score	159
					Team Place	6th
				82	Mark O'Bryan	18:49
				109	Mike Bruner	19:19

	1991				1992	
3	Jerry Kazlauskas	15:39		**1**	**Jerry Kazlauskas****	**15:27**
19	Steve Bair	16:35		7	Steve Bair	16:09
22	Jason Clark	16:40		20	Charlie Moore	16:34
26	Mark Lattin	16:46		22	Jason Clark	16:37
45	David Peyton	17:16		30	Derek Brown	16:52
	Team Score	94			Team Score	67
	Team Place	2nd			Team Place	2nd
57	Jeremy Kruger	17:29		67	Jeremy Kruger	17:28
84	David Clark	17:54		73	Kevin Bair	17:37

trails, **trials** & *triumphs*

	1993*			1994	
1	Charlie Moore**	15:11	1	Charlie Moore**	15:11
5	Steve Bair	16:00	6	Chris Lanham	16:01
26	Derek Brown	16:39	36	Brandon Swope	16:52
27	Jon Eriksen	16:40	52	Josh Skillman	17:08
31	Chris Lanham	16:46	60	Jerry Adams	17:16
	Team Score	73		Team Score	122
	Team Place	1st		Team Place	4th
32	David Clark	16:49	69	Seth Woodward	17:20
64	Eurel Maddox	17:22	122	Jeremy Myers	18:15
	1995*			1996	
6	Chris Lanham	16:40	1	David Christian**	16:25
9	Derrick Roby	16:49	8	Derrick Roby	17:00
12	David Christian	16:50	14	Jason McGuffin	17:10
13	Brandon Swope	16:51	25	Mark Rowe	17:35
16	Seth Woodward	16:56	45	Chad Kimberlin	18:03
	Team Score	50		Team Score	80
	Team Place	1st		Team Place	2nd
55	Robert McCann	17:41	49	Chris Matheny	18:06
66	Jason McGuffin	17:47	90	Robert McCann	18:34
	1997			1998*	
1	David Christian**	15:38	1	David Christian**	15:10
6	Jason McGuffin	16:23	2	Devin Swann	15:45
12	Mark Rowe	16:36	11	Mark Rowe	16:11
61	Chad Kimberlin	17:33	15	Chris Cox	16:25
71	Blake Main	17:41	28	Wes Aull	16:54
	Team Score	127		Team Score	54
	Team Place	3rd		Team Place	1st
94	Dan Riherd	18:04	30	Blake Main	16:56
105	Robert McCann	18:10	45	Jason McGuffin	17:16
	1999			2000	
5	Mark Rowe	16:30	8	Mark Rowe	16:05
21	Jordan Tong	17:11	15	Jordan Tong	16:15
22	Wes Aull	17:12	23	Andrew Adams	16:45
30	Daniel Riherd	17:18	32	Jon Richard	16:56
43	Jon Richard	17:31	46	Lee Cunningham	17:13
	Team Score	113		Team Score	115
	Team Place	2nd		Team Place	2nd
56	Lee Cunningham	17:43	67	Joe Collins	17:30
60	Chris Shown	17:46	78	Michael Cable	17:35

141

	2001			2002*	
22	Michael Cable	16:56	9	Michael Hunter	16:41
30	Jon Richard	17:00	10	Jon Richard	16:41
31	Lee Cunningham	17:01	14	Brandon Berry	16:46
42	Denny Weston	17:16	22	Trae Gaddis	17:01
44	Brandon Berry	17:17	23	Jared Keller	17:01
	Team Score	145		Team Score	73
	Team Place	3rd		Team Place	1st
63	Jared Keller	17:38	36	Drew Hawkins	17:15
100	Matt Rowe	18:06	50	Matt Rowe	17:30
	2003*			2004*	
11	Josh Yeckering	16:41	8	Tyler Stanley	16:34
13	Tyler Stanley	16:45	13	Drew Hawkins	17:00
14	Brandon Berry	16:46	18	Jon Dunaway	17:04
21	Trae Gaddis	16:56	25	Nathan Malony	17:16
32	Jon Dunaway	17:07	30	Trae Gaddis	17:21
	Team Score	88		Team Score	81
	Team Place	1st		Team Place	1st
34	Drew Hawkins	17:10	76	Wes Mobley	17:57
36	Matt Rowe	17:12	89	Josh Lockhart	18:09
	2005				
27	Jordan Payne	17:08			
52	Benji Whitehead	17:33			
53	Wes Russelburg	17:35			
82	Jordan Clark	17:57			
87	Jon Dunaway	18:00			
	Team Score	244			
	Team Place	7th			
102	Shane Powell	18:10			
105	Ryan Cravens	18:11			

VII

— Our Unsung Heroes —

"It must have been cold there in my shadow . . .
to never have sunlight on your face.
You've been content to let me shine.
You've always walked a step behind . . ."

The lyrics from "Wind Beneath My Wings" adequately describe many of the young men who come through our program. They never make a headline. They do not gain notoriety. They are out in the summer swelter and the winter freeze, faithfully logging the miles. Those miles can be counted in the thousands over a four year high school career. These young men are often at school for morning practice as the sun rises and get home late in the evening. They sacrifice time and other opportunities. Their running goals and dreams are complimented by blisters, aches, pains, sometimes injuries, and often disappointment. Yet, in many respects, these guys are the real strength, the heroes of our team. Some of these young men could have run varsity on most any other team in Kentucky, yet they came through our program at a time when the collective talent was so deep they were denied the chance to ever run a Regional or State Meet.

"I was the one with all the glory.
You were the one with all the strength.
Only a face without a name . . .
I never once heard you complain."

These guys have been invaluable to the success of our program. The old adage that there is "strength in numbers" is so true. Competition for their spot has always made our top seven runners stronger. Indeed, there have been years where our second seven could have qualified for State and had a decent team finish. Large teams, like large families, add to the memories, and I am thankful for every young man that has ever laced up his spikes for Daviess County High School. Each and every one of them have taught me something, made my life richer, and made their teammates better.

"It might have appeared to go unnoticed . . .
But I've got it all here in my heart.
I want you to know I know the truth.
I (we) would be nothing without you!"

Tons of thanks to the young men that have given four years to Daviess County High School cross country that fit the criteria I have described: Greg Jasper, Pat Riley, Neal Pagan, Brian Goodman, Derrick Wells, Jerome Johnson, Andy Hutchinson, Josh Johnson, Joe Revlett, Austin Swope, Keith Stallings, Nic Johnson, Devin Foster, Matt Anderson, Jay Barron, Brett Schrooten, Brandon Allen, Zach Day, Eric Hardin. To all of you and a multitude of other young men that were with us one, two, or three seasons, and have given so much to our program, I trust that it was all worthwhile. Words cannot express how grateful I am to you, our unsung heroes! The truth is we've been able to "fly higher than an eagle" because you have been the "wind beneath our wings!"

VIII

— Summer Camps —

In about 1981 we began having summer camps. There are some great cross country camps offered by universities and name coaches which provide wonderful opportunities, but they are very costly. Having your own team camp has many advantages. First of all, we can provide a terrific four or five day experience for around $100.00 per runner. Camp is a time when you can set goals and seasonal expectations. You eat, work, and play together. You get a deeper glance into each other's personalities, strengths, and weaknesses. It is a great bonding experience for the team.

There are numerous ways to go about conducting your camp. Years ago we roughed it in tents, usually at a state park somewhere in Western Kentucky. I was the chief cook, which meant pop-tarts and cereal for breakfast and cold sandwiches and beans for lunch. One day I had to open a big can of pork 'n beans with the claw end of a hammer because I forgot to pack a can-opener. A lot of guys passed on the beans that day! For supper, we would go to a restaurant in the area for some real sustenance.

In the early 90's, we began utilizing a church camp up in the hills of Pellville, Kentucky that actually had cabins, showers, a swimming pool, and cooks. Besides logging lots of miles, our activities included the "North American Diving Championships," the "Greater Pellville Horseshoes Open," and a camp biathlon consisting of 300 meters of swimming and a hilly 5000 meter run. It was very competitive, and we kept points on everything and presented awards on the last day of camp.

The last several years we have been able to really upscale camp. Bob Foster, who had an outstanding career for us, manages rental properties in the Pigeon Forge and Gatlinburg, Tennessee area of the Smoky Mountains. We have been able to stay in lodges that sleep the entire team and several parents. Three or four mothers do the cooking (they carry can-openers), and the dads help supervise runs and provide transportation. It is a great way to "camp," and we get the benefit of training in the mountains and enjoying the natural beauty of God's creation.

Whether tents, cabins, or lodges, having your own team camp is well worth the effort. Camp environments generate their own incidents, most of them good, and create great, lasting memories. Let me share just a couple.

Gatorade

In the summer of 2001, we stayed in Stonegate Lodge on a mountain above Gatlinburg. On the first afternoon, as the team headed down the mountain, the mothers mixed up some Gatorade and set it outside on the deck railing. They knew the guys would be thirsty, especially after negotiating the steep incline finishing their run. Before we returned, Donna Richard went back outside and noticed the canister was gone. Confused, she was ready to open the gate of the railing and investigate when an unusual sight startled her. Just a few feet away, a bear had the jug on the ground between its paws, and the big rascal was sucking at the spout, relishing the taste of the sweet fluid inside. Apparently, it had been a tough morning, and he needed to replace some electrolytes!

We kept a watchful eye after that, as our furry friend visited often during the next few days. We affectionately nicknamed him "Gatorade," and we still use that jug with his teeth prints around the spout.

The Creek, the Wedding, and the Moon

We stayed in Stonegate Lodge again for camp in late July '05. From Thursday evening through Monday morning the guys packed in about 40 miles of runs on beautiful trails, up and down mountains and through Cade's Cove. We always tried to plan runs so we could jump in a cool, rushing stream somewhere during the run. One of our favorite sites is in Greenbriar Park. At this particular place, the boulders in the stream form a natural waterslide over a current strong enough to be plenty of fun and a little dangerous, exactly what high school boys seem to like. We were in the water cooling off after our Saturday evening run when about twenty locals showed up for a creek-side wedding. We could tell it was a wedding because one guy (the preacher I presume) had a tie on and a Bible in hand. The couple didn't go to a lot of trouble to get dressed up, but the bride did have a nice wrist bouquet that identified her as the special lady of the evening. Our team continued frolicking, whooping, hollering, and having a blast. With the roar of the stream, most were oblivious to the sacred vows being exchanged about 50 feet away. Well . . . it happened! Somewhere probably about the time the preacher was getting to the "if anyone objects speak now" part of the ceremony, Shane Powell slipped and fell just upstream. The force of the water pulled his shorts (outer and under) down to the general vicinity of his knees as he headed downstream, flailing and tugging. His running trunks were completely swept off, and it was all Shane could do to get his underwear back up to cover everything that needed to be covered. I tried to give Shane all the encouragement I could to keep his "moon" from shining as he struggled toward the wedding party. Finally reaching the calmer water (right in front of the ceremony), Shane timidly sat in the stream and got things back in order. We never did find his running shorts!

The team plays in a cool, rushing stream after a run in
the Smoky Mountains during summer camp.

IX

— Training and Workouts —

Basic Training Guidelines

They say there are "many roads that lead to Rome." Numerous books are available that teach sound principles for effective training. Find them, study them, see what is best for your situation, and get after it. Without going in depth about cycles, energy systems, and such, let me share a few simple basics that we use in implementing training schedules.

We use a hard-easy pattern. We don't want to "bury" our athletes' legs, so we rarely run back-to-back workout days or a hard session on the day following a meet. We like to use Monday and Wednesday for workouts and Tuesday, Thursday and Friday as distance/recovery days. Many coaches use Thursday for their second hard session each week, but runners are a bit more rested for weekend meets by using Wednesday.

During the season, our freshmen generally run 35 to 45 miles a week and the older guys average 50 to 60 miles. We do double sessions three days a week which makes it much easier to keep up the total volume desired. The last two or three weeks of the season we cut out the morning run and drop our total mileage about 30%. It's important that the guys feel fast at this time of year, and the extra rest is a key factor. The team is encouraged to use their newfound energy wisely and cautioned to cut back slightly on their food consumption, since they are burning fewer calories.

One key to success is to get your athletes to realize they are runners; therefore, they run! There is an "aerobic age" (often referred to as background) that is key to consistent and fast performances. This is accomplished through year-round activity. It makes absolutely no sense for a distance runner to compete in cross country but not track, giving up that extra half year of training. It's like putting bricks on a house and then taking them back off, never quite completing the job.

At the end of each season athletes need a little physical and mental break. However, physiologists suggest that a well-conditioned runner may lose 15% to 20% of his max V02 (oxygen uptake potential) if he does nothing for three weeks. I read an article several years ago that suggested runners could retain most of that training effect by running every third day during their transition between seasons. That is exactly what we encourage our guys to do; take about three weeks of running an easy five miles every third day. It gives them time to recharge, and they are usually anxious to recommence their regular routine. In '98 David Christian ran the Footlocker Nationals on December 15th. He then followed the described pattern until the 3rd or 4th of January when he resumed his daily schedule. Just over two weeks later David opened the indoor season posting 9:20 for 3200 meters.

— Favorites —

Here are some of our favorite and most effective workouts, most of which have been borrowed from other coaches. Our goal for most of the sessions is to run very controlled with a "pack" mentality. The guys don't have to be fired up everyday, but they do need to realize that every session places another piece of the puzzle, and consistency is vital. All the early and mid-season core leads up to Red Line Training, which does require a meet type mindset, as we then bust it wide open.

Opening Time Trial

In Kentucky, we are allowed to begin team practice for cross country on July 15th. A few years ago, the late Rich Rostel shared that he began that very first day with a time trial. This serves the purpose of keeping the kids accountable in their summer training and gives the coach an idea right out of the gate as to the fitness level and commitment of each runner. We use two miles as our initial time trial distance.

Mile Repeats on a 10 minute Base

This is a nice workout for keeping the team together even when there is a wide range of abilities. We run 3, 4, or 5 x one mile runs. Every ten minutes another run begins. If an athlete runs 5:30, he has a 4:30 recovery. If he runs 7:00, the rest will be only 3 minutes, and so on.

AT Runs

We often use Anaerobic Threshold (AT) runs in the pre-season and sporadically after meets begin. They are done at a fairly high pulse rate, but still in the aerobic zone. We do these over three, four, and five mile runs with two different goals. One goal is to hit even-paced splits. For example, if a runner is 24:00 for four miles, each mile should be as close to 6:00 as possible.

The second type of AT run is with a descending pace objective. For example, the runner may have splits of 6:15, 6:05, 5:55 and 5:45 on his way to a 24:00 total. Our guys really enjoy the challenge of hitting their desired paces.

Continuous 200's

My buddy, Jeff Miller, shared the continuous 200's idea with me. We do 2 or 3 sets of eight 200 meter runs with a 200 meter jog between. In the pre-season, the fast 200 may only be about 40 seconds, but the idea is to push each 200 recovery. Later in the fall, the fast 200 may be around 32 to 34 seconds without pushing the recovery stride as much. Each set totals two miles, and the guys really like this workout.

200's

I have discovered through the years that 200 meters is an efficient distance for getting good effort from our runners. The distance is short enough that athletes can mentally "stay in the moment," even when doing many repeats. Late in the season we may go from continuous 200's to something like 16 or 20 x 200 with a standing interval of 30 seconds to one minute.

Continuous 5200

We begin this workout on the track with a 1200 meter run quicker than 5k race pace. Without stopping, runners jog a very deliberate 200 meters to a designated spot outside the stadium. Here they begin a two-miler on the roads at 5k pace. At the end of the two-miler they keep moving, jogging 200 meters back to the track where they finish with a very fast 400 meters. The workout correlates to the possible racing strategy of getting out well, maintaining, and then finishing with a flourish.

40–60

This is a good workout for getting or staying sharp. Although it can be done over varying distances or terrain, we normally go three miles on the road. Athletes will need a watch. Run 40 seconds quick . . . back down for 60 seconds . . . 40 on . . . 60 off . . . and continue the pattern until the distance is covered. Most of the time this is a very controlled run, however, we have had guys run as quick as 15:55, really pushing the 60 second recovery portion.

Continuous Kilometers

This session is done on rolling hills and turf, sometimes on our home course. We run 4 or 5 kilometers with an immediate kilometer jog and a 30 second stand between each. Four repeats add up to 8 kilometers; five, a 10,000 meter run. Add in the warm-up and cool-down and you come up with a very decent afternoon of mileage. We often divide the team into groups of seven or eight guys, according to ability, for the workout.

Lake Workout

Our home course has a lake encircled by a 500 meter path. We do a continuous ten lap session of up-tempo for 350 meters followed by a 150 meter jog across the dam on each lap. The total distance gives us a strong 5,000 meter run.

Ladder Workout

My high school coach, Bob Puckett, enjoyed putting his teams through this workout, part of which was on a long, gentle hill.

10 x 100 meters/:20 second standing interval
6 x 200 meters/1:00 standing interval
4 x 400 meters/2:00 standing interval
2 x 600 meters/3:00 standing interval
1 x 800 meters/rest 5:00

Finish with 10 x 100/:20 standing interval . . . or . . .
go all the way back down.

Popsicle Stick Runs

A coach at the Footlocker South Region suggested this one for a fun, yet very challenging afternoon. Give each guy on the team a numbered Popsicle stick. With stick in hand, each man runs out as far as possible until the coach blows a whistle at 60 seconds. Runners place their stick on the ground where they were when the whistle sounded. After a 60 second interval, they run back 60 seconds . . . trying to get to the original starting point. They do the same thing a second time. At the end of this (the fourth fast run), there is a two minute standing interval. Runners then go out over a prescribed course . . . six minutes one way before reversing the course (when the whistle blows) back to the starting point. This allows for all runners to be back very close to the same time. After a three minute rest, the athletes again do a 60 second run, trying to reach their Popsicle stick. They pick up the stick and, after another minute rest, run back for 60 seconds, trying again to reach the original starting point.

Having one of your team parents meet you at the end of the workout with popsicles would be a refreshing way to conclude this workout.

Red Line Training

Red Line Training (RLT) is actually a series of workouts that we picked up from Joe Newton of Elmhurst York High School in Illinois. It is an excellent sharpening tool for the important late season races. We do RLT on the roads, in race shoes, over courses that are meticulously measured for accuracy. The idea is to run much faster pace (especially in the one and two mile segments) than races. Most of our athletes will run personal best times over these distances during RLT, and it has a definite impact on their confidence at this critical time of the season. The work-outs are done on the last four Mondays of the season and are as follows:

Week #1:
2 miles (full out)–15 minute rest–1 mile (fast)–3 minute rest–1 mile (fast)

Week #2:
3 miles (full out)–15 minute rest–1 mile (fast)

Week #3 (Regional Week):
2 miles (full out)–15 minute rest–1 mile (fast)

Week #4 (State Week):
1 mile (full out)–3 minute rest–1 mile (fast)

Weights

"If all else is equal . . . the stronger man wins!" If a young man can improve his bench press from, say, 110 pounds to 130 over the course of the season (which a lot of distance runners could do), I have to believe the extra strength, along with the corresponding gain in self-esteem, gives him potential to run much faster. I teach a morning weights class and most of the sophomores, juniors, and seniors on my team are in the class. I can control both their lifting and the rest they need before impor-tant meets, and we have seen the benefits.

We are fairly aggressive with upper body weights and very careful with lower body lifting, realizing the legs are getting quite a workout every day through the miles and hills. If squats are going to be a part of your athletes' program, leg curls are also a must. Experts tell us that the quadricepses are naturally about twice as strong as the hamstrings. Overemphasis on squats, the most popular lower body exercise, makes that relationship even more off-balance, putting the athlete at higher risk for hamstring pulls.

Sample training week: mid-season

Monday: AM: 5 miles–light to medium
             Weights
             PM: Warm-up: 2 miles
             5 x kilometer/kilometer jog
             Cool-down: 1 mile

Tuesday: AM: 5 miles–light to medium
             Weights
             PM: 6 miles–light to medium

Wednesday: PM only: Warm-up: 2 miles
             2 sets of 8 x 200/200 jogging recovery
             Cool-down: 1 mile

Thursday: AM: 3½ to 5 miles–light
             Weights
             PM: 6 miles light to medium

Friday: PM only: 3 to 5 miles light with 4 x 100 meter pickups

Saturday: Race day

Sunday: 5 to 8 miles–on your own

Sample training: week before State

No two-a-days. Weights sessions are very light. Mileage is cut down about 30% to 40% from weekly average during season.

Monday: AM: Weights
             PM: Warm-up: 2 miles with 4 x 100 meter pickups
             Red Line Training–session # 4
             Cool-down: 1½ miles

Tuesday: 6 miles at light pace

Wednesday: AM: Weights
             PM: 5 miles at medium pace with 4 x 2:30 pickups
             during run

Thursday: 4 miles at light pace

Friday: Jog state meet course with 4 x 100 meter pickups

Saturday: State championships

"SWIFR"

Championships are not won just in the daily running sessions. Champions must be willing to do the small things that make a big difference over the course of a season. Champions incorporate winning habits into their lifestyle. This includes everything from what a person reads and thinks to who he hangs around with. I encourage my athletes to embrace five daily habits that can have a huge impact on their running. We call it the "SWIFR" program. Here they are.

S = Stretching: A bit of extra stretching each night goes far in helping a runner recover from his workout and prepare for his next run. Many runners have especially tight hamstrings and much attention should be paid to these muscles. As our athletic trainer, David Ralston, has said, "tight hamstrings are like running with your brakes on!"

W = Water: Since most of the body is composed of water, it makes sense that we need lots of it. Water is used in the body for digestion, elimination, transportation of nutrients; it is life to the body. Eight glasses per day are recommended, and what we get from food, juices and such is included in the count. Just a little racing tip . . . while sports drinks are popular and useful in replacement of electrolytes, they are designed for post-workout/competition. We prefer to use water for hydration in the hours leading up to competition.

I = **Ice**: We recommend that our athletes get Dixie cups, fill them with water and freeze them. At night while doing homework or watching television, they can peel the cups down and give tired muscles a very effective ice massage. The cold is great treatment for aches and pains as well as promoting recovery and preventing injuries.

F = Fruit: Fruit is unbelievable, powerful food. To list all the benefits of bananas, apples, and oranges would take pages. On top of everything else, fruits are relatively low in calories and easily digestible. Most young people snack on high sugar content junk food that has very little nutritional value. They must make a conscientious effort to include regular helpings of fruit in their diet. When that pattern sets in, the body will reap the benefits.

R = Rest: Teenagers are notorious for staying up late. They think they can somehow catch up on sleep missed. Consistent, regular bedtimes and sleep patterns will make a difference in practice, meet performance, and overall health. Another little tidbit of information that I impress on my runners is that the rest they get two nights before a competition is possibly more important than the night prior to a race. Think about it! Why do people dread Mondays so much. Many folks get plenty of sleep on Sunday night and still they are dragging around on Monday. Ask them what time they went to bed on Saturday night, however, and it is a different story.

So, if you want to be "SWIFR" than your competition, develop winning habits.

X

— Mental Preparation and Motivation —

I have often heard people say that distance running success is more mental that physical. While I do not completely agree with that thought, the mental aspect in running is extremely important. Coaches must be diligent in recognizing the emotional state of their athletes. Confidence, like fitness, is built on a slow-burner, step-by-step. Unfortunately, that self-assurance, especially with teen-agers, can vanish almost overnight. What follows are several ideas, some tangible and some intangible, that I use to instill that lasting positive psyche into our runners and motivate them.

Don't Compare

Don't compare to previous seasons, especially if "last year" was highly successful for the team or individual. Comparisons are futile! Every team and runner is going to have highs and lows. I warn our guys to get neither overly hyped nor discouraged over any single workout or race. Rather, keep emotions in check, and concentrate on consistency of effort. It's much easier to sail on smooth waters.

Have Fun

Motivation and mental preparation cannot be separated. An athlete who looks forward to practice and enjoys his team will likely give the daily effort required for success. Training day after day can become drudgery. Most young people who quit a sport will give the standard response of, "It wasn't any fun." One would think that winning itself would be sufficient incentive to keep kids engaged; however, the best coaches must continuously come up with gimmicks to both lighten the mood and make the cross country experience a high priority.

Integrity

An often overlooked factor to success is integrity. I really believe that over the months of the season, a team attitude develops. A multitude of factors are involved; effort, respect for one another, weekend activities, what athletes listen to and watch, how they talk . . . everything has an impact. When a team steps up to the line in the championship meets, that attitude will become either an ally or an enemy. I honestly believe I have had teams perform above expectations at state because of their collective integrity. On the other hand, I have had teams crack under the pressure of big meet situations because of a party type attitude that had gradually pervaded the team. Coaches should carefully weigh what they allow and disallow in team settings. People say you cannot legislate morality. Perhaps not, however, coaches can and should do all within their power to point athletes in the right direction, beginning with their (coaches) own behavior. We must continually monitor how athletes act and react in practice, meets, social situations, the classroom, in wins and losses; proper habits create desired attitudes.

Quiet on the Starting Line

I want my team to be friendly . . . after the race! Anyone who has laced up his racing shoes knows how it is on the starting line. Runners are notorious for comparing fitness levels, injuries, and race strategies in the moments leading up to the competition. For many, sometimes even among teammates, they talk themselves right out of a good performance.

Education

The best athletes are students of their sport. How many high school runners know who won the last Olympic 1500 meter final? How many know the story of Billy Mills? How many can tell you what their school record is for 3200 meters? How many know how to eat properly before a meet?

I have found that long bus rides can be especially fruitful plains for productive reading and discussions. My runners love to get hold of my clipboard. They want information. "Knowledge is power," and our athletes need to have running magazines, books, and other sources of information at their disposal.

At camp during the summer, I give each athlete a three ring binder filled with Daviess County cross country records, history, training explanations, inspirational quotes and poems, goal-setting sheets, emails and profiles from alumni, and a variety of other material. As the season progresses we add to the booklet. Over a couple of years, each runner has a nice keepsake and lots of educational and motivational tools at his disposal.

Daily Team Prayer

We have team prayer most every day, usually in the huddle at the conclusion of the workout. Often, one of the runners will lead it. There is so much emphasis on athletics these days that it can consume our lives and mess up our priorities. It is important for our young people to understand there is someone bigger than ourselves, and ultimately He is the one who deserves our very best, in every area of our lives. A very wise person has stated, "there is a God . . . and we are not Him!" Living beyond themselves will ultimately result in happier athletes and better performances.

Overnighters—before State!

We take about two or three overnighters before state. Athletes look forward to them, and some of the more memorable moments of the season are created during this time. The guys learn valuable lessons about sleeping, eating, and handling the excitement associated with road trips. If this schooling takes place only on your state meet excursion, young people are likely to make mistakes that could come up costly in performance. Experience makes a difference!

The Trophy Case

Trophies are great motivators. Every weekend our team has a chance to pick up a team trophy or even two if the jayvee squad is also competing. We no longer keep the team awards we earn at invitationals because we don't have room to display them. Instead, our runners take them home as teammates decide who deserves the prize each week.

We do, of course, keep the regional and state awards. Between the men's and women's programs, the cases in our school lobby are chocked full of meaningful cross country and track trophies, all of which are symbolic of very special days. Our runners see that hardware every time they walk the hallways, and hopefully, they realize that we can always find room for more.

Team Pictures

Above the trophy cases, our lobby walls are lined with large pictures of champion squads. Not only do our runners pass those each day, but so do other students, and practically every visitor to our school, whether they are there for ballgames, plays, teacher conferences, or whatever brings them to Daviess County. I watch as many guests will gaze at each picture, seeing if they recognize one of the many past champions. I have to believe that when our athletes come in as freshman, they too want to be a part of one of those team portraits that will always grace the walls of our school.

Hall of Fame

In one corner of our school lobby, right between the entrances to the auditorium and the cafeteria, is a large wooden frame which displays individual pictures of the Daviess County Cross Country Hall of Fame. Several years ago, we came up with this idea and decided the qualifications for induction. Basically, runners that finish in the top ten at state or are on the First Team All-State squad are eligible for induction. We, of course, made the honor retroactive and had 8 x 10 pictures made of each athlete initiated. Some of those photos were recreated from old newspaper clippings from the 60's and early 70's. The display is very attractive and presents a great goal for our runners.

Running (Coach) with the Team

There are many cross country coaches in our country that continue to train and running with their team has many benefits. I have discovered through the years that I am more in tune with the tone of the team as I run with them. I can influence packing and behavior, monitor effort, have one-on-one or group conversations; all of these extras take place on top of the reward of maintaining my own personal fitness.

I also serve as a target for the team. They like to beat me in workouts, although I do not present much of a challenge to the older guys now. A few years ago, when much fitter, younger, and faster, I was doing a workout of 16 x 200 with the team. Upon completion of the last run, Jeremy Kruger, still gasping for air, exclaimed, "I did it! I did it! I beat you in 15 out of 16 of those 200's."

"Way to go," I said. "You had a nice workout."

"I've been waiting for four years to beat you in this workout and I finally did it."

Then it hit me. "Oh, by the way Jeremy, I gave blood this morning."

I really had given blood, but he was still exuberant over his conquest. The point is, beating me served as a great source of motivation for Jeremy. Running with your team has its rewards.

One Week Shy?

Expectations are everything. Young athletes will not give a coach more than he demands. Our two main goals each year are to win the regional and place in the top three at state, and I tell the team that from the first day of practice.

I have figured out through the years that it is quite challenging to run well one race beyond your goal. Considering that, there are only a handful of teams that have a realistic shot at winning our state meet each year. Some may actually have the physical talent . . . but their main focus is the regional, and that tends to be a liability the next weekend. State becomes more of a relief or a reward than a meet to excel in.

I have seen the same scenario played out often in individual situations. Most of the young men and women that qualify for Footlocker Nationals are capable of a top 15 finish; some thrive there, but many really struggle. I really believe the difference is often in the mental approach of each athlete going into the regional competition. Those races are so competitive and it takes such an effort to advance, that the meet becomes the most significant of the year. It takes maturity to move beyond the pressure of qualifying to being prepared for an equal effort in San Diego, and that mindset must be ingrained many weeks prior to performance.

The point is, athletes must determine what their most significant meet of the year is . . . and not let the mental push stop short of that goal.

— Late-season Mental Preparation and — Peaking for State

At the end of the season, when runners typically are most fit, the difference often is their psyche. Hopefully, there has been an intentional, accumulating mental strength (personal and team) through the previous months.

A coach never knows what might touch a nerve (in a positive way) in an athlete. Therefore, in the final weeks of the fall, it is good to incorporate a variety of potential attention grabbers to help move runners to an elevated mental plane that corresponds to their physical sharpness.

Our last two weeks of the season is an intensified appeal to Daviess County tradition through handouts and videos highlighting our past regional and state success and e-mails from past runners. We also throw in a few "it's that time of year" specials.

Lake Jump

The lake jump is a conditional tradition that began in the very early 80's. We were hosting the regional and in the victory celebration that followed, I jumped into a lake on our course. That particular day was sunny and fairly warm; the late October water, of course, was quite chilly. Once a coach sets a precedent, the athletes expect it to continue. The lake jump has become my commitment and reward to our team each year that we win the regional, and some years it is *cold!* One year I really dressed for the part with my cow-print boxers, water-wings, flippers, and a tie-dye hat. Some of the guys have actually felt sorry for me on some of the more frigid dips; however, most of the time they would just as soon toss me into the water as look at me.

Race Plans

On the Thursdays before both regional and state, we work through written race plans. They cover several scenarios surrounding the race, everything from what the athlete will eat before the competition to what their thoughts might be going into the final mile. We ask them about their greatest fears and what they will do to deal with those anxieties. We plan pace and place goals. I copy these and give one back to each athlete the night before the race. The session and plans really seems to help our men get focused on their task.

Spaghetti Supper

On the Thursday before state, after the race planning session at school, we bring the team to my house for a spaghetti supper. The meal includes the best home-made rolls this side of heaven, made by my mother-in-law. It has been necessary for me to put a limit on the number of rolls each runner is allowed to eat because, through the years, it has become a competition. The team record is twenty-six.

After the meal, we watch a movie or race videos. Often, a former runner or two will call during the evening to wish the team well. When the guys leave they are full of carbohydrates and hopefully prepared for a good night's rest.

Ties

We pull out the neckties for state. The guys wear them to school on Friday. It makes them feel like a special team on a special mission. After jogging the course in Lexington, the guys dress up again for the evening meal. It seems to bring out a bit more manners and maturity in our runners, and the guys actually seem to enjoy this tradition. Try it!

— Mental Preparation Chart for Last Two Weeks —

Regional Week:

Monday:	Red Line Training.
Tuesday:	Review Red Line Training results.
Wednesday:	Review regional history.
Thursday:	Fill out race plan sheets.
	Possibly watch video of a past regional.
Friday:	Jog regional course reviewing race plan.
	Ties worn to evening meal, if meet is overnight.
Saturday:	Breakfast together at Cracker Barrel if the regional is in town.
	Regional championship race.

Tony **Rowe**

State Week:

Monday:	Review regional results. Red Line Training.
Tuesday:	Review Red Line Training results. Lake Jump.
Wednesday:	Regional video.
Thursday:	Fill out race plan sheets. Spaghetti supper at coach's home–watch inspirational movie or videos.
Friday:	Jog state course reviewing race plan. Ties worn to school and to evening meal. Share emails and messages from former runners.
Saturday:	State championships.

XI

— Concluding Thoughts —

Each and every day of our lives, we learn. Often, we don't pause to reflect on those truths. Many of the ethics I live by have been acquired or reinforced through this sport.

From cross country I have learned

. . . hard work is an honorable virtue!

. . . it is not the size of the gift God gives us, but rather how we develop what's been given that counts.

. . . my teammates were and still are my family.

. . . my coaches were heroes. They pushed and pushed and pushed to squeeze every bit of my potential into performance, not only for the sake of the team, but ultimately for my own benefit and those that would be in my world in the future.

. . . this sport will never leave me. It hasn't and it won't. Long after I retire from coaching, cross country will continue to impact my life because life is about competing. I will compete until the day I die. We all will. No other sport challenges a person mentally, physically, and emotionally quite like this one does.

I have learned . . .

. . . from the hills - some challenges loom larger than others and will test everything within you. Those "hills," however, impute strength and perseverance into you.

. . . from the intervals - I have learned to keep on giving the effort. Even when life knocks me down, I have got to get up, and go again. There are breaks in the tough challenges of life, but the test will always return. Just like an interval workout, I have to step back up to the line and embrace the next challenge.

. . . from the distance runs - life has it's ups and downs, but consistency in the long haul is everything.

. . . from the races - where else can a young person learn so much in a 15 to 20 minute span? In racing, I learned that giving my very best is where honor lies. I learned that I must respect every opponent, and be prepared for unexpected twists. I learned that fear is best overcome by the plan we call preparation. In races, ultimately, I learned that I "reap what I have sown," and that is a principle I must live by.

A Circle Complete

Viewing a tape of the '98 State Meet one day, I realized the connections that fuse folks together and have made our cross country journey so special.

David Christian, Devin Swann, Mark Rowe, Chris Cox, Jason McGuffin, Blake Main, and Wes Aull had just capped off the most successful season in our school history with a tremendous effort. Their teammates, just as much a part of the title, were ecstatic in the moment.

Little brothers Matt Rowe and Jon Richard admiringly gazed at their newly crowned role models, perhaps envisioning their own big day which would become reality four years down the road.

There was Derrick Roby, one of the heroes of the '95 championship squad, congratulating the new champs. Other former Panther cross country and track athletes like Scott Katchuk, Phil Hodges, Dean Roberts, and Don Moore mingled in the crowd.

Parents and friends, some veterans with our program and some newcomers, white-collar professionals to blue-collar laborers, soaked in the events that will be forever etched into great memories.

It never ceases to amaze me how the collective effort of a group of young athletes can so dynamically blend together such a wide range of people.

My oldest son Mark will be tackling his first cross country coaching job this fall at Campbellsville (KY) University. He plans to eventually host a college/high school invitational that my team most likely will participate in. Younger brother Matt is also looking toward a teaching and coaching career and may one day bring his own team back to compete at Daviess County. For all I know, one of my sons or former athletes may take the Raging Red Line into the next decade . . . and my cross country experience will have come full circle. I am truly grateful for each moment I have had in this wonderful sport . . . I consider myself the most blessed man in the world!

— Index of Names, Schools, Meets, and Places —

C

D

E

F

G

H

I

J

L

M

N

O

P

R

T

U

V

W

X

Y

T A T E   P U B L I S H I N G   *& Enterprises*

Tate Publishing is committed to excellence in the publishing industry. Our staff of highly trained professionals, including editors, graphic designers, and marketing personnel, work together to produce the very finest books available. The company reflects the philosophy established by the founders, based on Psalms 68:11,

"THE LORD GAVE THE WORD AND GREAT WAS THE COMPANY OF THOSE WHO PUBLISHED IT."

If you would like further information, please call
1.888.361.9473
or visit our website
www.tatepublishing.com

T A T E   P U B L I S H I N G   *& Enterprises*, LLC
127 E. Trade Center Terrace
Mustang, Oklahoma 73064 USA